Nan's Tails

At Hill House Farm

by Nan Gould

Best wishes

Nan.

Published by somersethistory.co.uk
10 Society Road, Shepton Mallet, Somerset BA4 5GF

Printed by Remous,Wyvern Buildings, Glovers Close, Milborne Port, Sherborne, Dorset DT9 5EY

ISBN 978-0-9558714-0-5

Cover photograph by Richard Stone
Cover Design by Alan Stone

The Background

Hill House Farm, as the name suggests, stands on a hill overlooking the city of Wells and extensive views of the Mendip hills. From the other side of the house we look out onto Glastonbury Tor and as far as the Quantock Hills. The farm has been in John's family from his grandfather's day, then farmed by his father until John took over. There is a further hill surrounded by woods and from there Wales can be seen on a clear day.

As with most places there is a draw-back and here we are very exposed to the bad weather. As gales blow we are the first thing that stops them so roof repairs are quite common. The year of exceptional snows, 1962, John and I had gone out for the evening unaware the snow was falling. Although only a five mile journey, which took ages of careful driving, we were unable to get the car up the final hill home. It was left at the farm gate for five weeks before we could move it. Where snow had been dumped over field hedges in great piles to clear roads it was still there in May.

The farm was a dairy farm with a cheese making business. Whey being a bye product of cheese was fed to pigs so about 600 pigs were also reared. There was also a flock of sheep. John and I were engaged and it was thought a good idea for me to learn cheese making skills which I did and found it most interesting. Whilst John cared for the pigs and did the field-work and his Dad was mainly the dairy-man. It was very full days and not with the labour-saving equipment we have today. It was hard work and long hours.

Ten years after we were married we took over the farm and John's parents moved to what was our house at the farm entrance. Although it was easier to be on the site from the farming aspect, adjusting from a modern house to a farmhouse with a temperamental Aga caused a few grumbles on my part. At least if a cow was calving we could hear what was going on and pop out of bed to check all was well.

Changes in farming were already taking place. To continue cheese making a pasteurising unit would have had to be installed and at a price of more than the farm was purchased for the previous year when the tenancy had been bought out, financially it could not be done. Cheese making ceased as it would have taken years to get the money repaid on the pasteuriser if we had gone ahead. Without the cheese making the pigs were greatly reduced and the market for them went. We concentrated on developing the dairy herd which with sheep seemed to be the way forward. The days were just as full and as John's dad wasn't having such an active part with the work so my tractor driving skills were put to the test to be able to help John with the crops. I was from a farming family but of level ground, here every field has some degree of slope and seemed very daunting to me.

With this small insight into our background the story now begins as we start our married life.

A view of Wells Cathedral and the Mendips from near Hill House Farm

The Start of it all

It was in 1963 that John and I married and worked to save in order to furnish our new home. Gradually the rooms were carpeted and furnished and the garden planted. John's vegetable garden was admired and friends went away with arm-fuls of produce as the new land provided rich growth to everything sown.

Both of us were from farming families so our lives had been devoted to the care of animals. Somehow the house and garden were still empty without any pets. Having been ill, in a moment of weakness I mentioned how I would like a dog. The next day my parents arrived with a dachshund puppy. It came on my Mum's lap, curled up in a ball, but as the puppy woke up, she stretched and it was like watching a concertina, hence her name Tina. She was a black and tan standard smooth haired three month old pup and she was the start of our household pets. As we accumulated so many over the years, with many amusing stories of each one, it only seemed right to share these.

Tina was aptly named as her length seemed to go on forever but she could sleep curled up quite small. Her feet were large, as in previous bygone generations dashshunds were used for badger hunting. She was very biddable and loving, giv-ing us a lot of pleasure in spite of a few chewed items as she grew up. Her hunt-ing instincts were still inbred even though dashshunds haven't hunted for years. Except when going to the farm, she spent all her time with me and at some stage during the day we would go for a walk; this was usually pleasurable but dachs-hunds never tire, unlike humans.

We would set off across the fields and possibly see a rabbit or two which was no great problem as they always made for their burrows if chased, so it meant Tina had a good run with no harm to the rabbit and I just casually walked around. This was not always the case as having walked around three large fields a fox popped up and off it went. Tina by now was in hot pursuit and suddenly deafness set in and I, some way behind, began to run at least to keep sight of the direction we were all heading. Some two and a half hours later we were home having been to the next village, around part of the moors and only giving in because she had lost the scent on the road. I was left apologising for a late tea and wishing I didn't have to cook, whilst Tina still raced around the garden in case there was some more sport lurking amongst the cabbages!

She loved the garden and whether it was because she watched us or she needed more vitamins, she would help herself to anything she liked. Peas were picked one pod at a time and brought back to the lawn where it would be popped and devoured. Strawberries were apparently good but the excitement of an onion had to be shared. She would eat the onion then eagerly come to us and of course we would bend down to make a fuss of her and get a full blast of onions as she returned her devotion with kisses.

Tina and Koko

As Tina developed, of course there was no better dog anywhere in our eyes, and as she had a long line of champions in her family we tried our hand at showing. Our local paper advertised a show especially for dachshunds at a town about fifteen miles away so we entered her in the appropriate classes.

Mum and I parked the car to see people leading as many as eight dogs each, so we knew we had it wrong with our one entry. This small show, as I thought, turned out to be the South West of England Show. Everyone seemed to know everyone else and their dogs so this odd bod and her pooch were getting some strange glances!

We passed the inspection then had to wait for our first class. Not having done this before, I carefully watched to see what would be expected of us. The novice class was supposed to refer to the dog but I was certainly also in that category!

There were four dogs in our first class and guess who was last and in the next class as well! Realising I was quite out of my depth, and not knowing the correct terms for different movements, I was all for coming home. However, our moment of glory was to come. It was our next class, so we went through the procedures yet again, and for some reason we were promoted to second place. Not a good move because when a very doggie owner asked me where my next show was I replied that I would not be entering again as it was not my scene, and was quickly told that I had only ruined someone else's chance to climb the show ladder by one appearance. With tail between my legs we came home vowing there would never be a repeat!

Visitors, until they knew better, or at least the ones we wanted to call, were very wary having knocked at the door and listened to the very deep bark before the door opened. Many were seen standing well back as they expected some huge creature to jump at them face to face, only to find this very short legged if long beast at my feet. Once inside an evening spent with friends would be enjoyed with no interruptions from Tina until eleven o'clock. Why we never did know, as we never went to bed that early, but she seemed to get the message across that it was bedtime. She would beg (that is sit bolt upright on her bottom with front legs dangling) looked the guest straight in the eye and yawn. Having got his or her attention she would move on to the next person, however many there were they all got the same treatment. Those that dared were treated to a second round if they hadn't heeded the first time!

Tina was two years old when John returned from the farm carrying a rather bedraggled kitten. There were no cats around at the time but huddled in one of the barns this poor little thing was to join our household. He was so pretty with a creamy yellow body and chocolate coloured ears and nose, but with eyes streaming and signs of a cold we didn't expect him to be with us for long. The vet was called to see to some cattle and he injected and left ointment to treat Koko, as he was now known. Tina was just finishing being in season so presumably her maternal instincts were in action. I did nothing to house-train Koko because every time Tina went outside Koko was picked up by the scruff of the neck and put down outside and not returned until he had been clean. Once back by the Rayburn, she would wash him and settle him by her tummy between her legs and go to sleep. She did this until Koko got too heavy so I weighed Koko and at that time he weighed three and a half pounds. Needless to say there was a lifelong bond between them.

It was 1966 when our son Kevin was born but there was no need to worry that the pets would feel rejected; they worked out a rota system to be with him. During the warm summer days Koko would sit under the pram placed on the lawn. He would come racing in to get me if Kevin cried, rather an unnecessary move as no one was in any doubt if Kevin cried! However, the cat always got a fuss made of him. This caring for Kevin was to last his lifetime, but more of that later.

The first vet's bill for Koko was not to be the last. On cold winter days he would jump on the handle of the airing cupboard door to open it and go to sleep on the shelves. One day we had a thunderstorm and he must have panicked as he wailed from the cupboard only to be found with a rather oddly positioned leg. We set off to the vets only to be asked to leave him and collect him later. He was given back to us complete with one leg in plaster and a bill of £14, which was a lot then.

We had a very large lounge so we kept him there as we were told not to let him out or get the plaster wet. It took him a couple of days to adjust to the weight of the plaster. Once balanced he could get about quite well with the plastered leg stuck out. Imagine my surprise one morning, in fact an autumn morning with heavy dew, to see Koko going across the field. I checked the door and it was shut but the

Koko in plaster

small window was open. To get out he had jumped up on the windowsill, then another jump of nearly four feet to reach his window of escape. Recaptured we let him stay with us as it was easier to keep an eye on him.

Three weeks went by and we went back to the vet for him to remove the plaster. Oh no it couldn't be that straightforward! The actual break had healed but bits of bone were poking through the skin so these had to be removed. With this done we returned home with instruction that the cat would be drowsy for the night and only a light plaster was in place to assist the healing. This so-called sleepy cat must have spent all night chewing and removing the plaster - it was in shreds and not a bit on the leg. Yet another trip to the vets for another plaster and the parting of £25. The next visit was the last for that particular injury. Little did we know that one year later we would have to go through the whole procedure when he did exactly the same again. All that behind him he settled to a more normal sort of cat life. Whereever Tina went, the cat was sure to be - but they were soon to be joined by another friend.

Lambing season arrived once more and as usual an orphan lamb was brought in to warm and be bottle-fed. Strong after a few days attention and taking a few wobbly leaps into the air, Tina and Koko took this newcomer out on the lawn. Koko watched this fluffy ball leaping and twisting in the air and he found it easy to join in, whilst Tina didn't really approve.

By this time Kevin was old enough to toddle around. It was very funny to watch the procession that followed him every-where. Two paces behind him Tina was first in line, followed by Koko at the same distance apart with Bimbo, as the lamb was now named, taking up the rear. If Kevin went right or left so too did they in this long line.

Kevin's odd sounds were now becoming words and he surprised us all by coming out with "Tia" as his first one, this he always used for Tina and she quite accepted it. It was his first sentence that was more surprising.

Tina and Bimbo

A friend who called most days was yet again greeted by furious sounds from Tina, inspite of the wagging tail. Only to hear Kevin say, "Tia might bite you" Never had we had to warn people about Tina, as there was no malice in her it was just a good display of protection. The only thing she really disliked intensely was a neighbour's bubble car. She became incensed as soon as she heard it. Kevin's limited vocabulary had us all foxed with his latest saying "der der". We heard it day and night but never understood what it was.

Following him and teddy at a distance I watched as he sat beside the hen's run and had this in depth conversation with them. Just stand and watch a hen, it scratches around and is 'saying' der der all the time. These hens liked this little person that spent so much time with them. They had many unusual experiences. Kevin could be seen wandering around with teddy under one arm and a hen under the other!

The hot summer called for a small paddling pool, which was meant for Kevin's pleasure, but the hens waited daily for their bath that he duly gave them! There were no protests whilst enduring this ritual. Embarrassment

Kevin and the Der Ders

9

was on my face when, having just provided breakfast for friends staying with us, Kevin enters the dinning room armed with a hen to clean up the crumbs!

What was an empty petless home previously was filling up fast. A visit to the local fair meant that, like hundreds of other parents, we returned with the plastic bag complete with goldfish. This fish had to be given a name according to Kevin. How many fish are named, let alone be called Humperdink after the singer? Needless to say he didn't escape Kevin's care so when he excitedly ran to me to tell me he had fed Humperdink I was rather curious to find out how he reached the food. On asking what he had given him he ran and got the pepper pot and on inspection this poor fish was swimming under this thick layer floating on the top. He escaped that ordeal and was lucky with the next one.

Changing the water was taking place in the kitchen sink when there were shrieks of "Humperdink gone"; yes you've guessed he had gone down the drain! One doesn't panic in this household, just simply go outside and pick up this rather bewildered fish from the grid of the drain and return it to swim round the now clean tank. His uneventful life continued until one morning he was on top of the water definitely dead. Recycling was not the mode then but Kevin's idea of disposing of this body was to take it out and feed this delicacy to the hens!

Having always had a pony as a child, with which I spent many hours a day grooming, riding or just enjoying his company, when I married he remained at my parents until he died. I missed him terribly, as I had never known life without a pony.

My parents comment on visiting them was to ask whether had I come to see them or Greybird? It was a great delight when my Dad said he had brought two yearling Shetland ponies. The bay one slightly bigger for my nieces and nephew as they were older and the small black one for Kevin. Hurriedly a piece of land was fenced off to make an enclosure - complete with stable, a converted hen house. The paddock was at the back of our house so many hours were spent watching the pony. Bosun arrived in a car trailer so you can imagine how small he was. He had been handled but that was all. It was too early an age to do much with

Bosun when he first came to us

him as he had a lot of growing to do. We did get him halter broken and could lead him about to get used to the many things that could appear alarming to a pony.

Being young he spent quite a lot of the day sleeping, always outside our kitchen window, often with his hooves up against the fence. Kevin would sit our side of the fence with one finger outlining the hoof as he recited "round and round the garden"! Kevin was unable to say Bosun so to this day he is affectionately known as Bobo. They became good pals and Bosun was introduced to bit, long reining and eventually a saddle. It soon became obvious this pony had no faults and would be completely trustworthy.

Bosun was about twenty months old when he was ready to try a little weight on his back, so we filled a bag with sand to try him which he accepted quite happily, so the next step was to get a rider who also was light enough - only Kevin. I led the pony and John had Kevin astride ready to pick him off if necessary. There were no hairy moments so riding was to start in earnest.

Very short rides were all that was allowed for sometime but eventually we would set off along the lanes to our neighbours. Bosun would be tied to their front gate whilst we had a squash then return home. This neighbour was breaking in a 15 hands high pony at the time and when fully trained we had great fun altogether. On Sunday afternoons Kevin and I would set off to her house where she would have her pony ready. She would ride and I would lead Kevin on Bosun and then she and I would swop. We went for miles like that.

Kevin eventually learnt to bump saddle at the trot and actually wasn't a bad rider so he progressed to the gymkhana circuit. We would turn up in a Landrover and cattle trailer John had made, which didn't look too glamorous, parked with the "in set"! Having explained the different events and quick practices at home we thought we were well on our way to Harringay or White City or wherever the right place was to be seen.

Musical poles were old hat but our first event was musical sacks. Well Kevin's drilling of sack-racing at home all became rather confusing to a two year old. Above the rest of the field noises Kevin's voice could be heard to say, "they haven't got one for me" so the kindly ring staff had a re-run to make sure all these really tiny youngsters and their thick mums knew what they were doing!

The fancy dress was our event. The pony was alright it only needed long boots, a bright shirt and cap, hoist up the stirrups, and Penelope Thelwell went racing. The crowds usually found it amusing but competitors with very intricate costumes were not always so amused. We never took these events seriously just did it for fun, but it was a delight to get the first rosette for a place.

During the time of Bosun's training a fox got into the hens by digging under the house and making a hole to enter. How do you explain to a toddler that the six hens he thought of as friends had been mutilated by another animal - two weren't even dead

Kevin on Bosun

inspite of having flesh ripped from them. Anyway, we overcame that obstacle and it was soon forgotten.

The hen house and run was not to remain empty for long as someone gave Kevin a black rabbit, and not knowing a lot about rabbits I was pleased that Kevin took charge of it. They would sit in the run together and the rabbit became quite fond of Kevin, which was more than I could say. The bad tempered thing would bite and claw me but Kevin used to take it for rides on his now discarded baby walker. He remained with us for six years before he too dug in under the pen and escaped. He was often seen but wasn't going to return to the life he had had, once finding his natural status. For several years after his escape there were black rabbits around so he presumably found more than his freedom!

A bad year

There were no new animals for a while and we didn't want for more as the demands of the farm, house and one small child took enough hours of the day but we still had time for the animals we had. Bosun was still being ridden and enjoyed. It was on a ride to the neighbours and enjoying the drink, as previously mentioned, that Kevin shocked us all by falling down in a fit on her kitchen floor. Bosun still tied to her gate, we drove with headlights on and horn blowing when necessary to the local hospital.

Once there we phoned John to collect Bosun and concentrated on what was happening to Kevin. He was semi conscious and would float off to sleep again so we were sent home whilst tests were carried out on him. His condition to us didn't seem to have changed when we saw him that night, although we were told there was no need for concern and he would be much better by morning. Friends asked us out at night, which we reluctantly did, and afterwards we realised what a long night it would have been without their good-natured thinking.

Next day the visit to the hospital was much better as x-rays could find no defects but a further visit to the children's hospital would be arranged. Kevin had to be kept quiet but was allowed home later that day. Keeping him quiet was not a problem for a week or more and we longed for him to show the old interest in things. Before the appointment came through for the specialist to see him, Kevin was forever getting tonsillitis followed by more fits, each time he got it.

Everyone gets their bad years and this was one of ours. It was July and Tina spent summer days outside usually laid under a shady tree. When it seemed she was out longer than usual I went to get her only to find she could only drag her back legs. Rubbing didn't help so I took her to the vet. The diagnosis was a possible slipped disc in the back or she had bruised a nerve. If the latter was the case there would be improvement in the next couple of days. She was in no pain but it was awful to see her.

The first day went by with no change and the second day the paralysis had spread to her shoulders. She was unable to relieve herself so had become bloated. She always sat on John's lap after he had finished his meals and in spite of her immobility she still made it known that was what she wanted to do even though it was to be the last mealtime spent with us. I drove her to my parents and she loved a car ride. She made it so much harder by taking such an interest in everything she saw on that journey. Dad took her to the vets for me, as I knew she wouldn't be coming back. I felt such a coward afterwards as she had been so loyal to us and I felt I had let her down when she needed us.

Apparently, due to the length of back, these dogs are prone to disc trouble. She would rush upstairs, which I never thought was good for her, but once at the top she would run at great speed to jump up on the bed to wake me in the mornings. Although she did this voluntarily with no encouragement, it possibly weakened the spine, we shall never know but she left us with many happy memories.

The next few days were long and glum but the appointment for Kevin to go to the hospital put things into perspective. On the morning an ambulance arrived to take Kevin to the specialist, which was, to say the least, awe inspiring to a rather wary patient. As we were driving ourselves it was thanked but turned away.

The experience at the hospital was very humbling. Although Kevin's problem had to be sorted out, I felt almost ashamed to be there with our tubby healthy child, even if he wasn't always like that. What some families had to cope with, with little hope of any change, left me with mixed feelings of despair and gratefulness.

Kevin by this time hadn't spoken for at least an hour, but it was our turn to see the doctor. This anxious child was challenged to beat up the doctor to see how strong he was. He was put on the couch and tickled and played without realising notes were being taken of his reactions etc. All this done we had to go to another department for some electrical tests, but not before Kevin was given a handful of jelly babies. Now completely won over the ordeal of wires attached to him was being done for the "jelly baby doctor" as he was referred to from then on.

The result of all this was to put him on medicine to try to stop the fits, which we now thought to be the effect of high temperatures due to the tonsillitis. More checks in the future and the tonsils would be removed when Kevin was seven.

We felt relieved that there was a remedy which, although not one hundred percent guaranteed successful, certainly offered a high chance of normal life. All this took place on my birthday, which was of little importance compared to Kevin's health.

Our riding friend called that evening to ask about the events of the day and mentioned she had seen some Dalmatian puppies advertised locally. This was a breed of dog I had fallen in love with as a child, but at that time they were few and far between. A quick discussion and a phone call and we all bundled into the car to see these pups.

We were greeted at this very large house with immaculate lawns and gardens and waited whilst the bitch was shut in, as she was very possessive of her pups. Some years later we were to hear she was not the most friendly creature anyway and met an untimely end when she bit her last victim which was one too many!

Seven pups were displayed in the house in front of us, whilst we asked various questions about their needs and what we were to expect from them. Some were more spotted than others and we were advised not to have a heavily marked one as the spots keep developing through their life.

One puppy was slightly smaller than the others and seemed a little more adventurous. She was quietly getting my attention as she only had five spots and being a bitch was also in her favour. Undecided we watched and chatted some more when the conversation was brought quickly to an end by shouts from the owner saying "oh my heathers, oh my heathers". Of course that was the winning streak for this pup that I was already warming to. She raced to and fro with this clump of heather and we made all the right noises whilst being shown the damage to the others but I could only admire the spirit of the culprit. The owner was quite willing to drop the price to be rid of this unruly monster, so bundled up we return to the car with puppy and looked back to see the garden being remodelled.

At home she cautiously ventured around the house and garden and met Koko who was indeed pleased to have a new companion. Tiredness was taking over this, as yet, unnamed puppy, so we left her in the kitchen and crept to bed ourselves, expecting to be disturbed when she realised she was on her own in a strange place.

Waking next morning, puppy refreshed from sleep, and possibly a private investigation of her surroundings, we were overwhelmed by such an enthusiastic welcome. Koko maybe remembering his own house training escorted the pup to the garden. She was rather surprised for the praise given for what happens naturally. All day ideas for a name were tossed around. There were no clues from the pedigree name, it was just too long. How or why or who suggested it I cannot remember but she was to be called Kim - good idea, couldn't be shortened or lengthened - or so I thought - but in her latter years she became Kimbo.

She was a good puppy and soon learnt what she could or could not do, but she could melt you with her eyes if she thought or indeed had done something mischievous before she got the telling off due to her. The only drawback was that her hearing was not good, something which is very often the case in Dalmatians. Watching her running around I also noticed she would jump aside as she neared an object. This was mentioned when at the vets for her inoculations, and the result was that she was quite short sighted. It didn't bother her as she knew the area, but in the fields if she

Kim

ran on some distance ahead of me, she couldn't hear any calls and she would look in all directions waiting for me to catch her up. Frustrating for both of us but there was nothing we could do about it and at least she just waited for me to get to her.

Koko would start the walks with us but would usually wait for us to be on our way home to join us again. There were various routes we could take, and if Koko wasn't to be seen on departure, he would be waiting to walk back with us at some point. This I found amazing, as I didn't know which way I would be coming home, but he did. Koko found the playtime with Kim was becoming more boisterous as she grew and he enjoyed it to a point, but, if it was getting too rough, one extended paw with claws at the ready soon brought it under control. Kim's spots were developing and helped Kevin with his counting as they were checked regularly to see how many more there were. It was good teaching, as Kevin was about to start school.

Working with farm animals means that anything that crops up gets attention, so although there is a basic plan for the days' work it cannot always be followed through. Kevin's going to school meant at least twice a day we had to work with the clock. Transport took him to school almost five miles away and he would return at about four in the afternoon.

Kim's walks were incorporated with meeting Kevin from the bus in the afternoon. She soon got the hang of this and if I didn't look as if I was going to leave soon she became very agitated. Three fifteen was the deadline to leave in her opinion because at that time she would run to her lead and back to me until I did go with her. This only took place Monday to Friday and if Kevin had holidays she was content to go out anytime during the day.

They were bred originally as coaching dogs that meant they ran with the coaches along their routes. Like Tina she never tired, always had boundless energy. She played with Kevin either with a ball or just romping around. She was a very gentle creature.

As with all children Kevin's top teeth were loose, in fact what held them in place was a mystery. They were so wobbly that it was whilst playing with Kim that she and Kevin both moved at the same time and bumped into each other with the result of the two teeth being knocked out. To a child that wasn't sure that nature would provide two more, he was not amused and it took a lot of convincing that they were ready to fall out anyway!

Kim showed a very caring nature to other animals, which was just as well because on a farm there are always weakly new born that need warmth and extra care. Lambs were often seen in a box by the Rayburn and being fed every two hours. It was not always successful but we farmers spend no end of time enticing something to live if born alive, and not obviously deformed, but just needing intensive care.

On one occasion one lamb was born prematurely, fully formed but very very small. Warmth was essential so I asked Kim to be in front of the fire and placed the lamb alongside her. She immediately tucked her legs around it and in no time both were asleep. She would lick it after it had been fed and having left the blanket by them, after one particular feed Kim covered the lamb with it to go outside.

She kept a constant vigil for nine days but on the tenth day she refused to have anything more to do with it. It had grown a little in those few days and looked bright enough but it was far from strong. Kim knew her task was over before we did as later that morning the lamb died.

Another occasion we had a group of sows not far off their time to farrow - that is to give birth. They all became ill and had to be taken off all food and given a water-based drug for two days. The drug arrived in powder form but instructions were given for liquid form. After a few phone calls we were advised what to do and proceeded to dose the sows.

The second day these pigs were behaving as if they had had a night on the bottle. Those that could stand and walk could only do so by propping themselves against the walls. Yes the translation was wrong and they had had the wrong amount but there was an antidote. These poor mums to be were in a pitiful state but did start to respond to the treatment.

Yet another visit to check the styes and there was an odd sort of pig squeal every so often. It was tracked down to one sow and by listening and scraping away the bedding two premature piglets were found, one alive, one dead. It was taken into the house in a box by the heat. Hourly checks on this particular sow found she had given birth to another live and dead piglet. Eventually we ended up with four in the kitchen. Being so early the sow had no milk and anyway had to concentrate on living herself let alone rear piglets. It took a while but the sows did all recover. Meanwhile Kim was licking the young ones and keeping her watch over them.

All animal mums lick their young not only to clean but also to keep the circulation going. As these four looked like balls of wrinkly skin it was surprising how well they fed and behaved like full time pigs. After the first forty-eight hours we thought we were home and dry but our hopes were crushed two days later when one of them died.

Kim and Koko quite accepted the farm animals encroaching on their territory as long as they could have a good look into the box to see what the occupant was this time! This was a bit of an uneventful stage in our lives, nothing out of the ordinary happened. This secure feeling was shattered when Kevin had measles, and some weeks later the fits reoccurred.

The next eighteen months were very trying as when Kevin slept he had difficulty in breathing and had to be kept in a sitting position. This resulted in John and I only sleeping alternate nights during this period. Finally the letter arrived inviting Kevin and teddy to hospital for the removal of his tonsils. We were obviously concerned, but selfishly the sheer exhaustion was able to take over. You have no idea how good it was to sleep every night as normal. The operation over, Kevin was still on medication for the fits but thankfully after four years treatment he was cured and was able to live a normal life with no restrictions.

The big move

Once Kevin was home from hospital there was a mammoth task to do. John's parents lived in the farmhouse and had decided it would be easier for us to swap houses, as often we would have to get up to see to a cow that was calving during the night. Although the move was no more than half a mile, everything had to be packed just as securely as for a long move.

The day was here to move. Well that was not just to take all our possessions to the farmhouse but to move John's parent's belongings to the house we were leaving. A couple of neighbouring men helped with the heavier items and by five o'clock both homes were full of furniture and boxes. The only priority for that night was to get beds made so after a quick dash to the local fish and chip shop, and a good bath the tired bodies were longing to rest.

The farm work had had to fit into this eventful day so every minute was taken up. Kim and Koko were the first to move in and Koko was shut in during the move, as we didn't want him wandering back to his home. A new paddock had been fenced off and the stable removed so we were all in one new premises.

When the rabbit deserted the hen house and run we did return to keeping six hens. We installed them in new quarters at the farm. They had the run of the farm after a few days, not necessarily the best move, as eggs were laid in the most unapproachable places such as on top of the straw on hay bales, room enough for a hen to squeeze into but not humans. Hens generally lay their eggs in the morning so they didn't get to roam until it was thought they had got laying eggs over with.

Most of these hens died from natural causes but one lived to be fourteen years old. She was used to wandering through the cattle but whether she made a mistake by entering the bull pen or just old age caught up with her we don't know but it was her last tour of the farmyard.

I was afraid Koko would wander back to the old house but he didn't. He and Kim soon got used to their new surroundings. Bosun wasn't in as close contact with us as he had been but surrounded by cattle he was quite happy. On one occasion his gate could not have been closed properly and a neighbouring farmer called in to say our pony was stood by the gate of our riding friend who had now moved away. The farmer had small children so he thought he would give them a ride before getting us, but Bosun was having none of it and stood rigidly where he used to be tied up.

Sometimes when bringing him from his paddock through the farm, I could see John needed a helping hand with something, so would throw the end of the halter over Bosun's neck and tell him he is tied up so don't move - he was always there when I got back.

Whether it was because of the new surroundings or not, but Koko became very protective of Kevin. At Kevin's bedtime the cat was always indoors, sometimes Koko would go up on Kevin's bed with him, sometimes he would only sit on the stairs and at other times stay with us. We got to understand the reasoning of this eventually. If the cat went to bed with Kevin we could guarantee Kevin would have a fit during the night, if on the stairs it would probably be next day and of course we longed for him to stay with us as we knew then all was well. He kept this going every night but as Kevin had less problems he would just go up with him and come down an hour later.

One night some years later he started to go with Kevin but came back and tapped his paw on Kim and kept doing it until she moved and he followed her still tapping her all up the stairs to Kevin's room. Of course once there she and Kevin were happy to curl up together. This pattern was to be repeated for three weeks which we could not understand, until one morning it was obvious Koko was not at all well. He didn't improve and sadly he died the next day. It was almost as if he knew and had to train Kim to look after Kevin. This she did until he was twenty two. It has been proved recently that cats can be good for epileptics as they can foretell fits. We weren't at all surprised at this revelation.

None of us were that concerned about replacing Koko, although he had given us a lot of pleasure we preferred dogs. However, Kevin had seen a black and white kitten at a local farm and the farmer was only too pleased to make one child happy so Kevin and Tinker came home. This new cat just grew and grew and when older would roam the wooded hill part of the farm to look for rabbits. People used to call in off the road to ask if we had lost a dog, as there was one wandering on the hill. They went away in total disbelief and thought we were off-handed when we said it was a cat! Just for curiosity we weighed Tinker and yes, he was big at twenty eight pounds plus! A typical independent creature, he liked to know we were there especially if it was feed time, but didn't take to being the pampered puss. He valued his territory and would often appear with war wounds.

At holiday times the cat population increased, as unworthy selfish people would bring their so called pet cat and dump it. We have seen as many as eight in one year, and it can't be coincidence they appear on bank holiday weekends. Presumably it was these cats Tinker objected to. He came in one day with a particularly nasty neck wound and we couldn't be sure it wasn't a mink bite. There are several in the area and they are particularly nasty animals as they don't just bite but hang on to their victim. This wound didn't respond to treatment and never did heal. One day Tinker didn't appear for his food, which was unusual, so a search in the farm buildings started. To no avail. We walked all his old haunts calling him. After several days we knew that we would not be seeing Tinker again.

Having mentioned the dumped cats, we can only be thankful that only one produced kittens. We did not know these had been born as they were hidden in the straw bales. When first seen they could have been about three weeks old and they were wild as could be. No mother was to be seen and the two kittens were hungry. Completely unapproachable, they spat, hissed and clawed. Food and milk was put for them twice a day and it wasn't long before they would be waiting for it.

Not confident yet of humans, they were reluctant to go to it whilst we were present. Eventually we won them over and could touch them, but unable to pick them up they had to remain a few more days on the straw. The black and white one gave in first and Kevin excitedly carried him to the house. It was the following day before the ginger and white one relented to do the same. Once indoors they were not the friendliest animals but with patience they gradually succumbed to this rather more comfortable lifestyle.

John played a major part in getting them quiet, as when he did actually get in to sit down in the evenings, he would have Tinker Two and Ginger on his lap. I was usually sewing or knitting so there was never enough room for two occupants. Kim, kind natured as she was, keen to have company again, won their attention by rolling a ball along the floor. This was watched for some time before it became irresistible and soon all three were playing.

Ginger was the 'gardener', if not to be seen she would appear as soon as John started work in the garden. She would roll over and want her tummy rubbed. As John hoed along the lines she went too. Tinker would only watch this performance from a distance.

A strange kind of growling sound was coming into the house and on inspection we found both cats were bringing in the smallest possible mouse. First one would carry it, then the other. We just watched to see what would happen. It was quite dead and very soggy but to our surprise it was brought in and put into their feed bowl where they just sat and rested after this big achievement. They looked at me as if they wanted me to share it out for their tea! Strangely if only one caught a mouse it was brought into the bowl all through their lives but if Tinker had the last one then the new one was Ginger's.

They used to jump in and out of a small kitchen window at will and it was nothing to come down to see a mouse in their bowl! They would be curled up together but would open an eye just to note if we noticed they had been busy through the night!

When Kevin started school it seemed a good idea to find an outdoor activity to get some fresh air and exercise. A local beagle pack, the Chilmark Pack, were meeting nearby so we set off. It was a good scenting day and we were hooked and waiting for the next weekend. We got quite involved and the owners were a hospitable family, always pleased to talk of the hounds to anyone interested.

As time went by the beagle puppies were fit for walking. For anyone not knowing the term 'walking', I will explain. Usually it is farming families that rear a couple or more puppies to introduce them to animals that they will encounter when working and not be distracted by them. They are usually good with cows and horses but sheep are more difficult as they always run when they see anything, which is very tempting for any pup. Well anyway on a visit to the kennels one evening we were asked if there was a chance of us taking a pup to walk, as it would be the only one left and didn't want it left in the kennel on its own not learning about the big wide world.

I knew exactly what the answer was going to be but found out a few facts of what it involved, I didn't commit myself but said we would talk it over. An old outhouse was quickly adapted to a kennel. Falcon was collected one Saturday morning and his first experience was on the way home. My niece was being a bridesmaid so we called by the church to see them arrive. The bells and cars were no problem and all the pleasant remarks were accepted. He didn't have time to miss his mates. Kim was pleased to welcome her new mate and was a great help to train him on the lead.

Once the new surroundings had been investigated it was time to go walking. Kim, complete with collar and lead, now to try the same on Falcon, expecting some jumping about and pulling back, but no, if Kim was going somewhere, so was he. Passing the first cows that he had seen at quite such close quarters he moved closer to Kim but kept going. As he was not to be a pet he was put into his kennel at night to sleep. On that first night anywhere would have done, it had been a busy day for a three month old, and sleep could not be put off any longer.

By day he was with me and went with Kim everywhere. His training to respect farm animals was fairly easy, as Kim showed no fear or desire to chase them, he got the message. The hens were a temptation as they always fluttered and raced around, eventually he realised that's just what hens did.

We took him on knowing it was just a short-term stay but as the day loomed for his return there were mixed feelings. I knew that his hunting instincts were not going to be suppressed much longer, which, in the area we live, could have been very satisfying for him. By parting with him he would be happy to do his natural job and we would be able to enjoy visiting him and watch him work.

It is impossible to have an animal for several months and not get attached to it. Stiff upper lip he went back to the kennels and settled in with his brothers and sisters; so from his point of view he was home. We missed him but with summer ahead there was plenty to do on the farm, so being well occupied helped.

Kim and Tinker had become great pals and spent a lot of time together and would curl up together when sleeping. Tinker went missing one day and there were frantic searches and calling. Ginger was quite lost, as she did rather tend to rely on Tinker for new adventures. She moped about all day and as night-time came we thought Tinker Two had met some terrible fate. The next day there was a very still atmosphere and sounds carried and were quite clear. Working in the garden in the afternoon I could hear the wailing of a cat. Listening to this noise and walking across a field it become louder. I approached a derelict building on the beams of which were stored some planks of wood and there was Tinker pacing on top. It was not high but just out of reach for me and it seemed as if Tinker had lost his nerve to jump down. I had to leave him to get a ladder, which caused him a lot of anxious moments as he thought he had been abandoned. We all three went to the rescue but his main objective was to relieve himself and then rub into us all purring profusely. Purring was something he rarely did, so we knew how pleased he must have been.

Ginger, not to be outdone, although didn't go missing, had to be rescued from the highest rooftop on the farm. She had walked along a wall then jumped onto the roof and settled in the centre on the ridge crying for help. John is not good at heights but the cat had to be got down, as she wasn't going to come back the way she came, however much we encouraged her. The height problem was overcome by entering the building, removing some tiles close to the cat, reaching through and retrieving her. She was very thankful and although she walked the wall she never tried the roof again!

Autumn neared and Falcon was going on his first hunt and we were there to see him. He spotted us but being a pack dog he stayed with his mates but there was recognition in his eyes, and much tail wagging. He was no fool in the field, his natural instincts took over and he was a good mover, so it was our delight to see him in the front group as they gave tongue. His clear black, white and tan markings were quite distinctive so he could be seen quite clearly. We saw him regularly at kennels and that was when we could make a fuss of him. He had done us proud at the pack puppy show, but if we could win the cup for the best working hound we would know we had it right, but we would have to wait until the next summer to know that. With all puppy walkers, everyone was sure theirs worked the best, but it was the hunt staff that worked with them that had all the answers to that. At least I was pleased he took no notice of any of the other animals in the field. The deer always ran away when he was here, and it was a temptation he had managed to resist!

The hunting season over but there were more pups and again we were asking to walk another. There was one dog with quite a lot of black, but the fawn marking was almost a grey fawn. He was a thinker, and would sit back with his head and body all wrinkled watching the others of the litter.

Politely I said I would take anyone that was left, as most walkers walked a pair, but I wasn't that brave! To our relief it was the little thinker that was handed over to us and his name was Dolphin. He was as sloppy as you could get and the very matter of fact attitude to life remained with him forever. Kim immediately swung into watching over her new charge and the cats tested him out and passed him as being no great challenge. As he grew the wrinkles disappeared, but he was not one to show great expression of pleasure or disapproval which endeared him to me.

That year there was an abundance of mushrooms, which I would pick when I walked the fields with the dogs. Dolphin soon realised what was happening so if he saw one he would sit beside it until I picked it. I did hope when hunting he didn't pursue this habit. Falcon knew what time we got up and if we were two minutes late he was the second alarm, but Dolphin wasn't the sort to get perturbed about anything, so there were no alarm bells from him. With this very laid back attitude my concern was for his future as he would have to show some keenness if he was going to hunt. Loveable animal that he was, there was more to life than that, so it was a great surprise on puppy show day when he showed beautifully and we walked away with best in show. He started hunting and, as we expected, he did what was necessary and was generally in the middle of the pack. He was no trouble in kennels and not one to push forward so not one to draw attention to himself either way, but happy enough.

Whilst with us, his brother a white cream dog, stayed with us for a while. He was being walked by my brother and sister-in-law, but through a stay in hospital, it was better for him to come here than to return to kennels then back to the farm again. What a different character he was, it made a mockery of the term 'walking puppies!' He was always on the go and could jump anything so I forever seemed to be running after this particular charge. He loved to curl up by the fire at night before going to his kennel - a big strong dog and made Dolphin look small. His stay with us was quite memorable and exhausting because of his mischief making.

Again there was a lamb to rear, this one though was not weak, it's mother ran into problems and didn't survive the birth. His everlasting demands for food never left us in any doubt what to call him, so Oliver it was! He drank his milk and nibbled everything in his path, whether it be grass, plants or shrubs, he had to be eating. He grew, needless to say, at great speed and wandered around the farm quite freely. We knew he wouldn't go far in case he were to miss that bottle of milk.

Eating our lunch one day we were startled as the outside doorknob started to turn, then even more amazed as Oliver walked in! Not content with that he climbed onto the sofa and laid full length to relax. This wasn't a one-off event and we would often

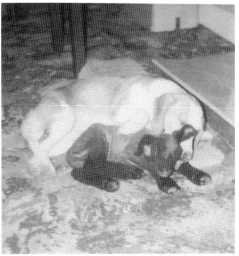

One of the beagle pups with Oliver

come in from working outside to find Oliver asleep, not only on the kitchen sofa, but the front room one as well! We were watching television one evening when in walks the lamb and he settles himself down in front of the TV and he thought that was marvellous.

From then on there was no stopping him and time after time he would open the door and race to the television and bleat until it was put on. Then he would lie on the sofa watching it! One nearly waited for his order for a sherry and nibbles from his lordship, but nothing was to distract him from his viewing! With two cats, two dogs and a lamb all muddled around the fire and on the furniture, it felt as if we were the intruders in their home.

When Oliver was first brought in the idea was to rear him for the deep freeze, but at that stage he had no character so it was no problem, but as this scrap of lamb developed into a fat woolly friend - his face was quite round and fluffy with just a black nose poking through - the deep freeze was not mentioned by any of us. He grew and grew and would wander with the cattle for a while then possibly visit the pony in his field, go to the hay barns with the hens before coming back to the house, so it was a life of sheer luxury.

Whilst working outside one morning no Oliver had bothered to see what I was doing, but I thought he was eating his way through a field somewhere, but strangely I couldn't see him, I did see the pick up coming along the farm track and the driver informed me Oliver would be arriving back in kit form for the deep freeze in two days time. The driver was nearly ready a lot quicker than that, but there was nothing I could do it was too late. True enough the joints did arrive and normally I love to eat lamb but these joints went round and round the freezer as I would only see that little woolly face and black nose haunting me, but it wasn't only me being sentimental, none of us could enjoy it.

The farmer is often considered a hard sort of person, but if you work with animals it's only kindness that gets results. No animal is going to put up with roughness without lashing out. If tone of voice can't get the response required, then you are doing the wrong job. Saying that, we see animal injuries and ailments more than most people who have other occupations. We do become more able to make decisions on how much treatment or suffering an animal can endure. Vets advice is always sought and the advice is valid but if it means the animal has to be destroyed, it is not something we like to have done, but at least it does prevent suffering. Talk to any farmer and however indifferent he may sound about his stock, there will always be a few favourites, and for some reason it's always those that has some misfortune and has to go.

The Chilmark Pack at the Midsomerset Show

Forager

On a happier note it's time for another beagle. This time we were to have a dog called Falstaff. He was big but he looked as if his coat was two sizes too big. He seemed to think he could use this size and if he thought he wasn't getting his own way would growl. It sounded fierce but that was all, he had no malice in him. He did all the usual things that the two previous beagles did and we were to walk six more in the next six years. They were all lovely and all had their own characters. The last one we had was a dear little chap but we were warned it was possible he would not be able to hunt, as his front legs were bandy. Someone likened him to a Queen Anne chair!

This little fellow was called Forager and he and Kim went through the same training programmes as the previous ones had. We took him to the owners regularly to check his legs. The problem was inherited but it was eight generations before Forager was last in the line. Certainly it didn't affect his mobility but it did look odd. His legs may have been is downfall but his facial expressions were so explicit.

During the winter we had a heavy snowfall with winds so there were some deep drifts. The lanes around this area had just got cleared enough for a car to drive or slide through. Forager had gone outside and sometime later I could hear him whimpering. On looking outside I saw him sat on a bright red patch of blood in the snow. The wind had blown a piece of glass onto the lawn and a jagged edge was just under the snow and had cut his leg. I quickly grabbed a towel, held it tightly around his leg then got Kevin to do the same as I drove to the vets. We slithered and slipped along the road and prayed nothing would come the other way. Kevin was telling me to put my foot down and I was thinking only fools would be trying to drive in these conditions. Eventually we successfully negotiated the five miles of road to the

Forager and Kim

vets.

We left Forager and the car and walked to the owners to tell them what had happened. They were concerned but so kind, I felt so awful, not that I wanted it to happen to any of our pets, but to happen to one I had been entrusted with gave me an awful feeling of guilt. There was no way of knowing of the glass being there, and the frightening part was wondering if there was any more, and where. We collected Forager, now cleaned up and having eight stitches put into the wound.

The cut had gone deep enough to cut the sheaths that the ligaments are in. He took no notice whatsoever of his injury and was as happy as could be. With unusual front legs and a sewn up back one, he didn't have much going for him. On the next trip to the vets the stitches were removed, and apart from a small line running across the leg, there was no indication of anything wrong. Obviously to a beagle its legs and feet are vital as when hunting several miles at speed are demanding. It was only a short time after when the snow and frosts melted that Forager was racing around again.

Both dogs loved the snow and in spite of Kim having a lovely patterning of liver coloured spots, out only a short distance and she would blend with the snow. It was very difficult to keep track of her, so it was good to know she would never go far away. One of Forager's paws had become very sore and I thought perhaps the frosty hard ground had caused it. It would not heal but we realised the foot dragged slightly and it was the result of the cut in his leg. We treated it for weeks and still it remained a raw patch.

The puppy show approached and the puppies should have gone back to kennels two months earlier, but thought it best to keep him here and keep trying to heal this foot. It was decided to forego the puppy show, which didn't matter, as the main objective was to get him hunting.

I did go myself to see the proceedings and came away embarrassed and ashamed as I was given the silver teaspoon with Forager's name inscribed on it, as is customary for all walkers to receive. These feelings were purely my own as there were plenty of enquiries of his well-being and sympathetic remarks.

The aim was not only to heal the pad, but also to get it hard to stand exercising for fitness and be ready for October to start the new season. Every treatment tried and still the sore persisted and the owner requested to see him again, this time to give us his final verdict of the situation. Pressing the sore didn't hurt, nor running across the lawn, but still the red sore remained.

Much discussion took place and it was clear Forager was not going to be fit for this season and if the pad was to heal the terrain that would have to be covered would not be suitable to a foot that wasn't hard. The owner thought if entered to the pack he would be most unhappy to be the one left behind on hunting days. The answer was to nurse him some more and an understanding suitable home would have to be found for him. With great restraint I agreed but it would be over my dead body that another home would be found, but wanted to talk it over at home with John. We related this outcome to him and there was no hesitation that Forager was staying here. Quickly a phone call was made and we were the rightful owners of Forager.

During the snow and severe frosts he had been allowed to sleep night times in the kitchen. It wasn't fair to be indoors with heat and with even lower temperatures at night to be shut in a cold kennel. All the puppies were let out for a run last thing at night then picked up and given a cuddle and some biscuit and left curled up on their bed.

Forager was no exception and now he was to belong to the team of pets he didn't sleep out in the kennel any more, but there was no way he would walk back into the house. He had to be carried and have his cuddle, and that he kept going for the next thirteen years. Like Tina his hunting instincts were very strong and he would go along the grass with his nose down, and if the tail started to wag, it would be too late to stop him and he would follow the trail.

Wildlife is plentiful in this area; rabbits, hare, fox, deer and badgers are frequently seen. To try to quell his desire to hunt, also to prevent him doing more damage to his foot, he was kept on a lead for walks in the field. It was funny to watch Kim's big strides covering the ground, whilst Forager had to take three strides to her one. He soon learnt that as Kim ran round, to catch her he had to cut corners; in spite of the difference in size they played well together. We would still go out with the pack at weekends and take the two dogs as if we were walking, they may as well be exercised at the same time. At all times they were kept on leads and, presumably because Forager had never been part of the pack, he never offered to "speak" as they ran past in full cry.

We had walked his mother several years before and she had a weakness for whisky. If ever there was a bottle open she would behave as most dogs would for a bone. One evening a friend was sat with a glass in his hand casually on the arm of the chair and he was in deep conversation. Freckle had popped up and was lapping the contents of the glass. She had only had a couple of licks when I shouted out; she had it in her mind to run across the room and jump up into a chair. She would run towards the chair take off, only the legs just would lift off the ground and she landed in a heap. After the fourth try she abandoned that idea and slept it off on the mat for the next hour or so, it didn't stop her liking for it. Luckily Forager hadn't inherited this liking.

The cats and the dogs all got along together and on winter evenings there would be a cat either side of Forager in front of the fire. Forager had a very odd way of lying full length with his back legs out behind him, he spent hours like that. His foot took months to heal and the new skin took a very long time to harden but he never favoured it. He loved his food and anyone else's if possible; so to overcome him eating the cat's food it was put on top of a cupboard, where they could jump up but out of his reach. Kim had a stainless steel bowl for her food, but as it wasn't intended for Forager to live out his life here, he only had a plastic one. Now he was part of the family he was all for equal rights! They were fed at the same time, but he would not eat his food and just watched Kim at hers, then when she had finished drag her bowl along towards his. I put his bowl into hers and he would promptly eat it so the next shopping trip was to buy a stainless steel bowl, from then on they both ate at the same time.

He loved playing with a ball with Kim, but because of her height she was able to get the ball to bounce away from her as she let it go. Forager would watch this and try as he might it would only land at his feet and this disappointment could be seen in his eyes and he couldn't get that envied bounce. I found an old sock and put the ball in it, well the delight in his face as it left his grip and went half way across the lawn had to be seen. This new toy was a great treasure, though indoors we were often the target of this flying object.

Hot air balloons frequently cover this area and he seemed to be able to spot them when so far away they looked like ping pong balls in the sky. As soon as noticed one he barked and frantically ran up and down the lawn for as long as it took to be out of sight. It didn't matter if we shut him indoors, if he could see it he wasn't giving in until it had definitely gone.

On the side of the lawn we have a tennis court, which we used a lot, on one corner there was one small gap above the wall that the surround wire didn't reach.

Forager would jump onto the wall, pop through the gap, as soon as a ball touched the ground he would dive in and get it and race around the court and back onto the lawn with it. When all the balls were gone we had to walk round to pick them up to continue the game. You could tell how seriously we played but we enjoyed it. Ageing limbs and creaking bones have put a stop to that pastime now!

One very wet morning had finally given in to a more pleasant afternoon, so off I set to take the dogs for their walk. Having just got off the farm track onto the road, I noticed a puddle with a bird in it. He looked like a small magpie from a distance but it was the wrong time of year for them to be about. The dogs were told to wait whilst I neared the puddle. The bird didn't move so I picked it up thinking it must be damaged in some way to let me do that. On closer inspection it revealed webbed feet - well I had never seen anything like it!

Two dogs that were used to long walks followed me home very dejectedly and the bird was put into a cage. We tried it with various titbits but it showed no interest, and we couldn't find out what it was. It was after some phone calls that we phoned a bird garden some miles from us and given the description we were told it was an auk from the Falklands. Helpfully they would send someone from our local town to confirm this. In the meantime we had found out he was happiest in the bowl of water and would just sit there. Sure enough the bird was identified and the RSPCA were called to take it to a nationally known rescue centre not far from us. Shops were shut this time of night but we were advised to feed raw fish overnight and he would be collected in the morning. The only fish I had was fish fingers. This was an odd substitute but he did eat it.

Knowing a reporter we rang her and told her how far this bird had flown and she wanted a story, asking what sort of thing it was, and gave her a run down of its markings and told her it was an auk. She came next morning, complete with camera, and was taken aback by what she saw. She explained amid much laugher she didn't think there would be anything special about a hawk and nearly decided she would not follow it up. She couldn't understand why I had dropped the "h".

There had been gale force winds, which the birds had got caught in and had assisted their four thousand mile journey. During the same week some were found at Bournemouth, another in Wiltshire. Duly next day the auk was collected looking somewhat brighter after a good rest. His travelling was not over as the next week soldiers were going to the Falklands - it was just after the war there - so the auk hitched a lift and was returned to its rightful habitat.

Of Pigeons and Ponies

John had always had an admiration for pouter pigeons, so an old stone building in the garden was made available. A wire framework was built out the front so that they could get used to their surroundings before being let free. This was also done to ensure they would return to cover at night time. Six were installed of various colours. They stayed inside but eventually cautiously they had to venture into the wired area because that was where their food and water was.

The time came when they were very sure of their house so we put a large bird table just outside of the caging and opened the door. It took sometime for the first one to make his escape to the table provided. Five more soon followed and they did look good all on the edge, heads back and chests out.

They would fly off but always came back to the table then in for the food. We had a lot of pleasure watching them and wondered how they could stay in what looked like a painful position for so long.

Passing the kitchen window one day I noticed two lying in the cage and one on the floor outside and on investigation they were dead and judging from the noises inside something awful was happening to the others. An animal jumped out of the house and ran so quickly it was only as it clambered up a nearby wall was I able to recognise it as a stoat. It had done its damage, none of them survived and we all hoped the stoat didn't for long.

After a while, and with no sightings of the stoat, we introduced six white doves into the house; they too were shut in until such time as considered safe to release. They were very distinctive and flew in huge circles around the farm. They were apparently happy as the six multiplied to an overwhelming number, but nature being what it is, the buzzards from the woods got the numbers down to a manageable amount.

It was during this time a racing pigeon landed on the roof of their house. We get a lot rest here and thought when his strength regained he would go on, but no, each morning he would still be there. The doves seemed to accept this newcomer and fed and slept together. 'Charlie Pidge,' as he was called, would eat from our hands and would follow us whilst we fed the farm animals, picking up a few titbits along the way. He stayed with us for several years then we missed him, but as we had no idea how old he could be we thought he must have died somewhere.

Nine nights later, Kevin had been put to bed as normal, but an hour later a little voice sounded at the lounge door saying "there's a funny noise in my room". We all listened to nothing, so about to settle Kevin down and convince him there was no need for alarm, there really was a noise and we all heard it.

We tried to locate it and decided it was in the chimney but as three chimneys are built together and it was dark, there was little we could do until morning. Knowing Kevin didn't have a runaway imagination he slept with no more interruptions.

The next morning I returned from a nearby town to see a friend's car parked outside the house, as I entered voices were to be heard upstairs. John, Kevin and the two friends had the contents of a built in cupboard stacked on the floor of Kevin's room. There was a heap of rubble, a square cut out of the room wall and a hole in the cupboard wall, all because the noise had been heard again. I had returned in time to witness the culprit of the scratching noises. To our utter dismay in the hand of a very grubby arm was Charlie Pidge. The first thing he did was flutter his wings and a cloud of sooty dust filled the room. He refused food but did he enjoy a long drink! It was lucky that he chose the bedroom chimney to fall down, as that hadn't been used for years. At a later date it was covered over. None the worse for his adventure, he returned to the outside world and his normal life until old age caught up with him.

The pigeon population had increased yet again and where as we started with white doves, we had a lot with various amounts of grey feathers. Attracting more pigeons from the nearby village when their owner died, they would drop in exactly at 8.30am have breakfast, and return to their home. Gradually it must have dawned on them there was no feed put for them at home so they just moved in. They would line up on the barn rooftops and all colours, but it was obvious with their prolific breeding habits somehow they had to be thinned out. At night perched on the eaves of the cattle house it was easy to climb to them and pick them up. The person that wanted them was somewhat taken aback to find the first catch was over thirty. Buzzards and owls were then able to keep the numbers to a reasonable quantity. After several years they died out, mainly because the magpies were taking the eggs.

You must be wondering why Bosun has not been mentioned for a while, well he was fine but Kevin kept growing and Bosun didn't. Shetlands can pull their own weight but not carry it. He used to give other smaller children rides but for Kevin, riding Bosun was over. The bond they built up over the years must be very strong.

In the early days when the pony was young and full of mischief I would go to the field to catch him, and just as I got to him he would canter around the field. After several attempts and with other jobs waiting, it was maddening but had to be overcome. On one particular day he just was not giving in so I went back to the house and got Kevin. He was about eighteen months old at the time. We walked into the field and, although Bosun was at the far end, he came straight to Kevin and we put the halter on and led him in. Kevin was used for this purpose for the next couple of weeks until the pony got out of the habit of being naughty. Even to this day, and they are both thirty one years old, if Kevin is spotted around the buildings as I lead Bosun to and from his field, there is no way the pony will move until at least Kevin calls out to him. Depending on what Kevin is doing at the time, he may leave what he is doing and start to walk towards us and the pony goes straight to him. If Kevin is on the tractor but just calls out "hello Bobo" he then moves on to go to the stable.

For a Shetland pony he does make us wonder how he would have survived in what should have been his natural habitat. It only has to spot with rain and he runs for shelter, and he will not walk through water. When Kevin used to ride, the only fault he had was he would always walk round water and not through it. Snow he will paw out to find grass, and that's not a problem to him. It must have been Kevin playing with his hooves in early days that makes an easier job of cleaning Bosun's feet. If he is lying down I just sit with him and do his hooves one by one, and he doesn't offer to move. Of course he is not always laid down, but still picks up a foot as I bend down then the next one is ready by the time I move to it. He knows exactly where all the cattle food is kept and as he usually trots to and from the field halterless, he stops to check that there might be the odd bit dropped ready to pick up. His converted hen house stable was now rotted by the weather and age, a new home had to be found. Five block built sows houses complete with a cement floor outer area were empty so it was one of these that we used for him.

Another we used for hens, we thought we would try again and beat the foxes. Bantams were introduced as they lay during the winter, and in any case they are prettier than hens. The only problem with bantams is they lay a nest of eggs and become broody, and if the nest isn't found they sit and incubate them. They are generally good mothers and that is why they are used to hatch pheasants and other

Kevin and
Bosun

both aged
25

types of eggs.

One duly sat on her eggs and I let her get on with it, as the older ones wouldn't be laying much more, so it seemed a good idea to have some chicks. The given time had passed, and one chick had hatched and we waited that day for more, but that was the only good egg in the batch. So mum proudly brought up the one but unknown to me, one week later another mum had hidden her nest in the hay, and appeared with one chick.

Two mums and two chicks were a nuisance so the second chick was put with the first one. The hen immediately took charge and put her wing out to cover the newest arrival. A week later a friend, having heard of the bantam and two chicks, arrived with a newly hatched chick. The hen was a clumsy thing and had killed the other but they managed to rescue this one. We took it to the mum with the two and popped it in under her, and straight away she was making suitable sounds that only a chick understands. As it had taken more than a fortnight to get a family together, it did look odd as one was nearly feathered, one had the first wing feathers and the other just a ball of fluff. They all survived even if the old hen did have to watch one going on too fast and one trailing behind, otherwise the age gaps made no difference.

Mrs Duck

The seasons play a large part in whether the eggs are fertile or not. Sometimes the hens will not even become broody or else very late in the year then the young don't always survive. We had a few ducks and it was a bad year for hatching them. Only one hatched out of twenty odd eggs, it was not very lively so in by the Aga it came. Kim and Forager would sit by the box and the cats showed a passing interest! Later the same day thirteen bantams hatched.

We put the duck with the bantams and they all grew up together. The duck fitted in well, the only problem the hen had with the extra different youngster was when it rained, she would take them in for shelter but baby duck wasn't going to co-operate and miss the joy of the raindrops falling on her. As they matured the hen left them to get on with her own life but it was the duck that took over the mothering. They had quite a daily routine. After a tour of the yards, scratching any cattle food that may have been dropped, by 10am precisely they would have got to the sheep dip.

After the season of sheep dipping, the water and chemical used for the sheep are drained out but rainwater fills it up again. All stopped for the duck to have her swim whilst the thirteen bantams stood in a line along the side and waited, this would take a good half hour, then more walking around the farm. At exactly a quarter to one they would come across the cattle grid onto the lawn. This was all right but Mrs. Duck, as was called, could not negotiate the cattle grid.

She stayed the other side making quacking sounds whilst the lawns and gardens were scratched and the occasional worm made their trip worthwhile. That done they would roam the fields until time to go back into their house for the night.

I'm sure Mrs. Duck could count because she would stand outside the door and call for them to go in. Any latecomers and the calls became louder and wouldn't cease until all were accounted for. When laying started with this brood they all sat and waited patiently by the next for the eventual clucking that meant it was time to continue their ramblings. The fuss Mrs. Duck was making one night time was particularly noticeable and really convinced us she could count, one of her family was missing, she called until darkness fell when she was coaxed to go inside with the ones she had. It turned out the missing one was sitting on eggs.
One afternoon all the poultry were squawking and that meant trouble. Usually at

this time of day they would be in their house, but looking inside revealed the horror taking place. A fox was attacking a cockerel but Mrs. Duck had hold of the fox's tail and was shaking and pulling it to try and free her adopted sibling. The fox eventually seeing and hearing me, scrambled onto a beam. Wondering how to separate them was the next problem, but catching sight of a long handled shovel, action started. Keeping an eye on Raynard, I scooped up a bantam on the shovel and put her outside. This was repeated until all were removed, the fox was shut in until John and Kevin returned from the fieldwork which had taken them away from the farm.

The poultry scampered to buildings, which offered some safety, but still the fox had to vacate their premises. We thought it would just bolt as soon as the door was opened for its escape, but it just sat on the beam. We shouted and banged and we waited and at last it broke for freedom, and the noise with dogs barking ringing in its ears, it didn't return for a second visit. Nervously the poultry returned that at night to be shut in.

The security alarms were buzzing and with a glance at the clock I knew it was the time for the entry to the lawns, but Mrs. Duck was making a much different quack, she had realised there was a flat strip in the centre of the grid and she was crossing it, rather like an gymnast walking the beam! She proudly glanced in my direction and burrowed her beak into the soil. This obstacle overcome she was able to join the gardening party daily.

The idea of keeping ducks was to fatten them for eating. Mrs. Duck was supposed to be no exception, but when of age to provide us with a meal there were so many excuses why it wasn't convenient to prepare her for the table that or the next week. When she turned out to be such a personality, it didn't get mentioned anymore. For eight years she cared for the bantams but yet again a fox passed through the farm one afternoon killing her beloved family. It was an awful task picking up the savaged bodies, but there was one missing. It was two days before we found Mrs. Duck's unmarked body, she must have had a heart attack as the turmoil was taking place. Any sympathy for a fox runs a bit thin in this area, taking one for survival is one thing, but to be so destructive and not take one at all or even eat a mouthful is not acceptable.

Like a lot of people, we prefer to see hens scratching and wandering about freely and we hear of cruelty caused by keeping them in all the time. The few we had certainly enjoyed their freedom but what was more cruel, than to watch one of the group being massacred knowing it was their turn next. Magpies would take the eggs as soon as they were laid. Crows would take young chicks so there is a very stressful life for the hen whatever way it is kept. We did make a covered wire pen with house to keep some in so that they were safe, but it wasn't very satisfactory so poultry are not kept here any more.

Living in a rural area with woods one expects foxes to be about but there are plenty of rabbits for their needs. We have seen a group of foxes early in the morning and a vehicle driving away at speed. We know these foxes have been brought from a city not too far away. If only the 'do good' group could see what they have done they might have reason not to do it. Town foxes are used to noise and the shelter of buildings, but dumped in a silent open space they are terrified. They have no idea where to go for cover and probably never had to catch their own food as a dustbin has always been inviting and rewarding. If we could only be at the scene when the foxes arrive ready to be released the people doing it might be educated about the way of country life! I suspect they are the sort of people that spout a lot of nonsense about protecting the fox, not knowing the grief it can cause the poultry farmer and the shepherd. They want it protected but not in their back garden. Foxes are pretty to look at and we often see them with cubs and it is fascinating to watch the parents teach their young, but being vermin they must be controlled at some rate, if we are not to be overrun with them.

Geese either breed prolifically or very badly, and it was a bad year when a friend gave one to Kevin, which was the result of the year's breeding. Like the hens it was tucked under an arm and carried about most of the day until it became too heavy. Having been chased as a child by a pet goose, I had reservation about this one. It grew rapidly and although he would puff himself to full size and make threatening hissing sounds, he didn't seem too bad, but I didn't trust it, rightly so as it turned out. With adult feathers he was able to fly and could often be seen circling over the fields. On one occasion someone was walking across the farm track and the goose was approximately one hundred and fifty metres away, the approach was not heard, but grovelling on the floor the poor fellow was rubbing his head and wondering what had hit him in the back of the neck.

He only had one more attack before it was his turn; prepared for the table and duly cooked we waited for the serving of the meal. He must have been laughing all the time as tough wasn't a big enough word to explain how much chewing had to be done to devour this meat. Warmed in a different way for the next day's meal, nothing would tenderise the meat. There was no more goose rearing!

Humphrey Hare

Tinker, Ginge, Kim and Forager, having the run of the house and being pampered at every whim, were not expecting life to alter when a new member of the household was installed. John and Kevin renewing a fence in the fields noticed a young leveret in the grass. Between banging posts into the ground and nailing wire they kept a watch on this small hare. It didn't move far and when it did one back leg was either damaged or deformed, as it had difficulty with its movement. Observation was kept on it at a safe distance and they thought the adult hare, though not seeing her would be doing the same.

At lunch time they returned for their meal then resumed work with the fence. The leveret was not to be seen not until they worked along the hedge to where they were able to look into the rhine. The water level was quite high and with a second look the leveret was in the water, definitely not a happy hare. They pulled him out and put him on a tuft of grass where a watery sun could shine on him. At the end of the work in the field and to be back to do milking, the parent hares hadn't been seen all day. After some discussion they decided this poor little chap was only going to deteriorate or be some night hunters supper. Surrounded by badgers, mink and foxes this seemed more than likely.

The animal world is very hard with a lot of species, if there is a weakly youngster, unlike ourselves we would do everything to tempt it to live, but if it is weak or deformed, it is more than likely to be left to die. We have proved them right on many occasions with the farm animals, when a youngster seems to want a lot of care yet the mother shows no interest she is usually right, it is beyond survival. Anyway this handful of fluff was passed over to me for care. Warmth was essential but it was so small it must still be suckling. Gently warmed milk was put into a syringe and thumb on the end just to ease it through, the hare sucked the other end hungrily which made me think he had been deserted.

Humphrey's first days

41

Sleep and feeds were the pattern for the next few days then we introduced grasses and clover. The Aga - an oil filed cooker - also provides heat for the kitchen. Placed beside this cooker are shelves, and that is where Humphrey hare would stay on a blanket. Strangely this was next to Forager's chair. They could both be seen sleeping so close, yet beagles hunt hares and Forager would in the fields, but because Humphrey was one of us he was welcome to stay.

Now this wild animal, showing signs of recovery, would have to learn a few house rules such as cleanliness. A box was provided the moment he woke and he was put into it and not allowed to leave until the paper was wet.

He soon got the message and on waking was told to go to his box, which he did but with childish mischief he sometimes would bounce out and round the kitchen, only to be told no play until he had been in the box, he would always oblige and I liked his spirit.

We were so used to Humphrey being on the shelves we didn't think of it being odd. A visitor sat chatting in the kitchen nearly choked on his coffee as he shrieked "you've got a hare on your shelf". When I calmly said "oh yes, Humphrey go to your box" and he stretched and obliged the order. The visitor sat there in disbelief and wondered what he had in his coffee! After the appropriate time Humphrey was told he could leave the box and to play, and disappeared with Forager and Kim. The poor chap was by now convinced he was going quite mad and hoping it was us.

It was as the daylight was fading that he really came to life and would run and leap from room to room shrieking as he went. When stronger he included the stairs in this exercise whilst this went on every evening the dogs sat in chairs and watched in amazement at this strange behaviour. By day, the waking hours all three spent together. If the sun shone through the windows Kim would lie in the warmth with Forager slightly away from her side, his back legs outstretched and Humphrey also

Humphrey and Forager

42

full length beside them. As the sun moved round, Humphrey would get up and bang his front paws on the dogs until they moved into the sunny space, and all settled down once more.

Humphrey's house training was faultless until he tasted sugar. Normally the sugar bowl was left on the table as the coffee is always at the ready. But we had to change that habit because the height of a table was no obstacle to a hare. One leap and he was there and the sugar bowl would

Humphrey on his shelf

be emptied. Why he had this obsession was hard to work out, as it would be alien to his wildlife diet. Chocolate buttons were another favourite and shredded wheat was always in demand. He was grown up and the box was not required anymore and first thing in the morning he went out with the dogs and learnt why they went out.

To a stranger it would look odd, the two dogs going through the door followed by a hare, then squat on the ground and return to the house together. It had to be seen to be believed that this wild animal was so used to the domestic life. If I was working in the garden he would be there with me, and the big green fields held no appeal. Never once did he use his claws, which were so sharp and long.

If John sat down in the evening, he quite often had a cat or two and Humphrey on his lap. In spite of being an adult hare, maybe it was to be treated the same as the dogs, but he always insisted on his bowl of milk. He spent most of his time with the dogs but the cats were sometimes treated to his company. The cats were always bringing rabbits in but it seemed as natural as could be to have a hare with them.

We learnt a lot about hares and were privileged to have so much pleasure from Humphrey, but it was only sixteen months that we had him with us. It was early morning and let out as usual, but a lot of low flying racing pigeons went over and Humphrey panicked with the noise and speed of their wings. He ran full length of the garden and over the fence into the fields. We took the dogs over the fence and called him hoping the dogs at least would coax him back. It was a long miserable day with many fruitless searches.

Night-time was nearing and Humphrey, never having had to defend himself the concern was how would he react if approached by a fox or badger. I left a trail of my working clothes, hoping he would follow it back to the house where all the doors were left open. No joy so we thought we would not see him again, a predator was bound to have had him. Walking the dogs next day we stumbled across Humphrey but having found his natural surroundings he was not going to be coaxed back to the house, even though he played with the dogs.

Every day we would see him as he remained in the same field and armed with his favourite titbits he was pleased to see us. This went on for six weeks then one day he didn't appear, but we left his chocolate and shredded wheat in his squat, it had gone by the next day but I wasn't sure Humphrey had been the one to benefit from it as he still hadn't been seen.

It is a well-known fact that if you have rabbits you will not have hares in the same area. We knew this but obviously Humphrey didn't, and must have strayed into the rabbit's territory, as it was a sad day when Humphrey and a rabbit were both found dead on the road. The time Humphrey had with us was a bonus as he would surely not have survived at the time he first came to us, but man cannot beat nature and sometimes it seems quite brutal but the different species have their own rules, and they have no time for intruders. He was greatly missed, especially his twilight capers, but by now we knew it would only be time before there would be something else turn up, as the first desire for a pet had apparently made it an open house for others.

Cows and calves

The farm animals take care of the greater part of the working day. For a cow to produce milk she has to have a calf first, this is not always straightforward. A healthy cow can go down with several illnesses within a few hours of calving, or even just the calving itself can be a problem. Sometimes it's the calf that needs the attention. The minute it is born it can be hit by several infections and if not caught quickly, it doesn't survive. Not all cows are blessed with a maternal instinct so their calves have to be hand reared unless there is a willing mum ready to take on the task.

It is distressing if a cow has a dead calf and this can happen for a number of reasons, some cows really mourn their loss whilst others are none too worried. We had one very large heifer - that is a young cow - due to have a first calf. We knew the expected date for the calf's birth but were taken by surprise when she produced one fully formed, active very small calf one month earlier than expected.

It was really sweet and strong in spite of only being fifteen inches at the shoulder. Being that small it meant there was no way it could possibly reach mums milk supply. We humans, with the aid of a bottle, overcame that and she stayed with the cow to look after her, and we just fed her. All of the first day we were mystified at the size of this calf because even at eight months of pregnancy it should have been bigger, but it didn't matter, as Mini Moo would grow. Imagine our astonishment when two mornings later Mum had given birth to a second calf, but that one didn't survive. Mini Moo grew into a normal sized cow eventually, with no defects at all.

We had a very bad calving time. One year there was an infection that hit into the calves as soon as they were born. All farmers that year had the problem and a lot of calves were lost. We had one under a heat lamp trying to will it to live when all the odds were against it. We treated it with the solutions left by the vet but it got so weak but didn't give up, it scoured, the farmer's word for diarrhoea, and lost its hair from its tail and rump. We would turn it every two hours so that it didn't get sore and it went on for days.

It was an Easter Sunday and I said I would make arrangements to have it put down as I felt it had tried to live long enough and it wasn't fair going through so much. Well I was completely taken aback, as when I neared the calf it was trying to get up. With this reprieve I decided to go to the local chemist and get some diarrhoea medicine, as it didn't seem worth spending vets fees on anything so hopeless. The chemist opened for an hour on Sundays for emergency things so there were a fair few people waiting. As I asked for a large bottle of the requested remedy, they showed me the normal size that was sold and I promptly said I would take four. The customers waiting all stood to one side for my departure, and after such treatment I didn't have the heart to say it was for a calf. Two doses, and with a little help, he was able to stand even if it was a bit wobbly. He never looked back from then on.

After feeding I would walk Hercules, it had to be called that, we watched him gain strength and walk about for a while. As he grew stronger the quiet stroll was getting faster and longer and a few skipping like steps were thrown in. After a while, with good signs of recovery and warmer weather, he was put into a small paddock with green grass underfoot. Our little strolls became full blown races. I had to join in or else I got a wet milky nose nudging me in the back. It is never good to make too much fuss of one animal that is part of a group, as they always expect priority and the others resent it.

At six months old, and still playful, we decided the time had come when some hard decisions would have to be made on his future. A cattle buyer came to the farm for animals due to be sold and spotted Hercules, he fell for him straight away and wanted him. We explained all about his past but he still wanted him. I called him and he raced to me and straight into the lorry. It may seem hard hearted but as he had got big and strong, and his nudges were getting rougher, he would have ended up by knocking me over and once down he would have been in control and could have done me quite a lot of damage.

He never played with anyone else in the same way, so we knew he would be all right in that respect. He lived his life quite happily in his new abode with no signs of roughness to humans, and being with other cattle he would soon have learnt the codes on conduct.

He was not the only calf to respond to treatment of that sort. We had another one at a later stage but not quite as ill to start with. Weak he was, but gentle exercise was essential to get those muscles working. Gaining strength the strides got longer and faster, with a twist of the body every so often. When let out it was like watching a rodeo performance, hence his name Rodeo, aptly as this routine was gone through every morning. He too never looked back once on the road to recovery, and grew into a fine beast.

It does give us a boost to get results like this as sometimes, through no fault of ourselves or any other farmer, we all get a run of casualties. It is not the financial loss, although that shows at the end of the year, but it does demoralise us when we think we have done everything best for their welfare then get fatalities. When we feel really sorry for ourselves we question why we do this but there is nothing else we know or want to do. It is not always the animals that come off worse as John found out one Easter Sunday.

It was a beautiful sunny day and with the sun shining into one calf shed they all pushed towards the gate for the warmth. With so much pushing, somehow the gate opened and freedom was too good to miss. Having wintered indoors as soon as they are let out cattle run wildly, and are carefully put into a selected area, where they can do this with the least risk of injury to them. These particular animals were unattended as they broke free and ran across a yard and straight into a manure pit. With previous rain it was deep with sloppy contents, and once in prevented them from moving about. Luckily I was taking the dogs out and spotted them, and knew this had only just happened.

John quickly went for a tractor to hoist the calves out, but the one for this purpose had the manure spreader hitched onto it, and in his haste he didn't go through the normal practice of lowering the stand for safety before unhitching. The release of the hitch allowed the drawbar to drop on John's foot. The stone it also landed on gave enough room for him to pull the foot away, and because of the severity of damage the numbness allowed him to pull several animals out before neighbours arrived to assist. With pain and blood seeping through the boot, which we quickly removed as swelling was occurring; we set off to the hospital

The neighbours saved the remaining calves and John stayed at the hospital whilst I returned to the milking. Some clever stitch work saved the severed toes, but it was six long weeks before John could wear boots essential for work. Being physically fit and being unable to get about was very wearing for everyone, but thankfully at the end of the six weeks his walking was not impaired.

At that time of year the land needs rolling and harrowing and with good weather the animals go into the fields so John couldn't relax. But in a small community although we don't see a lot of the neighbours, given a crisis everyone pulls together and this was no exception. Obstacle overcome we settle down to the normal routine and the farm hasn't been neglected, but with the main person out of action the repair of machinery and jobs of that nature didn't get done, otherwise all else was under control.

Naughty Mr Bun

Kim, Forager and the cats resigned to the fact that Humphrey was not going to return, all four would spend a lot of time together. The cats still brought the mice in, but if it was still alive, the new game was to drop it in front of Forager to get him to join in the fun - if that's the word. What is more callous than a cat torturing a mouse?

A new responsibility was soon to be theirs again. Kevin carrying a woolly hat and a great big smile, was thrilled to hand over the smallest rabbit to replace Humphrey. The hat was his home for several days and the syringe feeding was resumed. Two dogs always hoped it would be a messy job and were waiting for any drops of milk that may go their way. The foster carers licked the face of the rabbit when feeding was done before sleep took over for Mr. Bun. He was growing quickly but much harder to train than the hare, and no matter how much John tried to encourage him to be friendly, his only reward was a very hard bite. If you haven't ever been bitten by a rabbit be assured it hurts.

At about a month old a bantam was busy hatching some chicks. The hen was so pleased to sit on the eggs but as the chicks hatched she would throw them out of the nest. They went into a box to go indoors to keep warm, as she was likely to kill them or they would die anyway. If the chicks dry quickly they don't go fluffy and it just dries in clumps and won't fluff until the actual feathers the clumps away. Mr. Bun was sat in a chair and, I thought, a nice warm body which wasn't too heavy that would keep these chicks warm and make them dry and fluffy. I popped them in under him and he seemed to know he had to stay still. With one nestled under an ear, and two more unseen somewhere beneath Mr. Bun, they emerged sometime later all dried and fluffy. Saucers of food were prepared for the chicks but Mr. Bun couldn't resist joining them, after all they were his chicks.

Mr Bun and chicks

The dogs and the rabbit all got along well together but Mr. Bun wasn't the kindly natured animal that the hare had been, and as he got older his biting habits had worsened. One day he caught hold of Forager and just hung on making Forager cry out with the pain.

From then on there had to be some changes, as the rabbit couldn't be trusted anymore, so he was put into the conservatory and only let out with us and the dogs in the evenings, when we could keep an eye open for fair play. He would bounce into the room where we were and jump into a chair, or on the hearth rug, and roll onto his back and would do it on instruction for his tummy to be rubbed. He would let me do anything with him but he was quite savage with John.

Mr Bun did race around the room and leap onto John, which pleased him to think he might be trying to be friendly, but he would then jump off either leaving John with a wet lap or bite as he leapt, or just for good luck do both. He would tolerate Kevin if he respected his moods.

During the day, weather permitting, he was put into a large run on the lawn. He started by nibbling at the grass, but he learnt how to dig. Holes became bigger and deeper; it was fascinating to watch, as it was a very purposeful task. Once able to get into the mouth of the hole, earth was dug at a furious rate and when enough soil was loosened, it was piled up then he would push it with his nose and pat it down until it was level. This was a natural thing to do but in case the hole came up on the outside of the run, I would call him to check he was still there and sure enough, after a couple of times of hearing his name, a rabbit in reverse would emerge.

With the moving of the run the lawn was like a minefield, as although the holes were filled up, they would sink, so humans did plenty of twisting over of their feet. He did sometimes dig himself out of the run but was always spotted. His quick and jerky movements drew attention to himself. He would stop if called so it was easy to catch him.

Given a Wendy house it was placed between the lawn and garden and it became Mr. Buns new home. It meant everyone would

Mr Bun and Forager

now use the conservatory without risk of their ankles being bitten. I always felt anyone trying to break in through the conservatory would quickly be discovered by the screams, as a couple of sharp teeth would sink into their leg. He wasn't always bad tempered; we had a lot of fun with him. I say him, but we never did know if it was male or female.

Mr Bun and Tinker

The cleaning process was a very lengthy programme. First the front feet were cleaned of mud by pulling it off with his teeth; they were then licked and rubbed together. When clean and inspected they were used to wash the face. Satisfied that was clean, the neck and back of the head were next. Time to do the ears, the ear was held with one foot whilst the other one did the cleaning then change the feet over for the other one. It took quite some time to do this, but the rest of the body was done in the same meticulous way. Once completed it was time to skip and twist - that was a leap into the air and twist a number of times before landing. A friend tried desperately to get this on video but Mr Bun never co-operated when he was here.

It is quite amazing the amount of food a rabbit can devour, collecting the various greenery was quite enjoyable as it became less easy to find during the winter. The dogs thought it was good because it meant a longer walk. The best thing was that the garden was kept free of weeds, as he liked most of them in his diet.

He lived quite happily in this way and escaped the dreaded myxomatosis that swept through the area, but his death came quite unexpectedly when he was eight and a half years old. He was left at night with fresh food as usual, but next morning when I went to let him out, he was going nowhere as he had died during the night. It was a shock as there was no indication he was unwell but at least he had no suffering.

Life begins at …

Kevin left school and I had my fortieth birthday and was gearing myself to this myth that life begins at forty. Well yes it did, but my idea was that the workload would become somewhat easier now that three of us were doing the work. It was the time that big round bales were being brought into farming, so we got a baler and Kevin did some contract work. After the first summer of this it became the in thing and the contract work snowballed so two were at home again. The phone was going non-stop and the bookwork had to be done, none of us had dreamt it would become a full time business. It was a few more seasons before the bales were wrapped in polythene instead of putting them into bags. John got a wrapping machine so then of course both of them were gone all day.

Kevin's first successful summer over, and winter ahead the cattle were brought in from the fields, which means they have to be fed and houses cleaned daily. Well into November and John was unwell, but thinking it was a dose of flu and that everything would grind to a halt if he didn't do his share, he kept going even though he looked and felt awful. On the third day when his neck became swollen, he did give in and go to the doctor. A blood test was taken and he had to wait three days for the result so he was advised to take to his bed, which by now he gladly did. The results of the blood test didn't come soon enough as it was obvious it was more than flu, and it was.

Glandular fever was diagnosed. Asking all sorts of questions about how long and what to expect, I listened to the reply in disbelief as John always shook illnesses off easily, so why not this. No medication is prescribed as it only has a bad reaction. It really has to burn itself out. For the first six weeks he hardly knew he was with us as he just slept, and the pain in the neck glands were so painful he couldn't bear to shave. He couldn't cope with visitors, as pleased as he might be that they called, it just wore him out. Christmas came and went with Kevin and I sat down to a thirty-four pound turkey, which looked a bit stupid but it would have been a houseful in normal circumstances.

Gradually John was able to sit with us for an hour in the evenings and he gradually built it up but if he overdid it he was so weak it would mean another full day in bed. While this was going on, Kevin saw to the feeding and cleaning of the cattle, whilst I did the milking. Those poor cows were my outlet, they knew exactly how I was feeling but also it just got me out for a few hours a day. If it wasn't for

John being ill I was in my element keeping calving records. I knew the cows, when they calved and how much milk they were giving. It was so interesting that it was easy to be in another world when with them. I had always loved milking as a child and can remember climbing onto my father's lap to start the art of hand milking. At five my proudest possessions were a milking coat and stool, and the faithful old white cow that put up with my then long-winded extraction of her milk.

It was sixteen months before John was able to get back to full time work so it was like learning to identify the animals anew.

He had tried to do jobs on the farm but would tire so quickly and had to give in, which physically did him no good and of course he would become miserable and wonder if he were ever going to be fit. It was a long and difficult time for everyone but at least it was curable even it took ages.

Raring to go again, the memories of the last few months fading, they were back in business with baling and wrapping silage. The demand by now had grown so much that, weather permitting; they would start at five am and possibly finish at midnight. The makers of the wrap held a competition for the person who wrapped the most bales in a season. It was a bonus John needed to win and in due course a rather luscious hamper was delivered. The competition was withdrawn the second year, as three contractors would have held the same positions for years to come.

Kevin was in demand for performance articles of the baler to advertise the make he used, apparently one report was written in several languages to advertise in a worldwide magazine. It was considered that during one season a baler doing his amount of work was the equivalent of sixteen seasons. With glee the makers thought that was great but Kevin having the last say said, "the machine is only as good as the operator" and in fairness that too was quoted.

Maybe John needed to take it easier but John was always trying to keep abreast with the modern trends, and had been following with interest information on a new breed of beef cattle being introduced to this country. The Belgian Blue cattle have double muscles and therefore are huge. The BB Society held a six monthly sale at Chelford, so off John went.

The show was held on the Friday followed by the sale on the Saturday. A phone call on the Friday concerned me - he was hooked! He remarked on the marvellous animals there and on Saturday he returned triumphant with his purchase of one white bull. Admittedly he was a superb specimen and although very large, as quiet and docile as anyone could hope for. At the time the cost of the bull was astronomical and my dreams of a retirement bungalow seemed even more remote now. The sale report had been on an early morning farming programme and radio so the first visitor arrived during our breakfast, to see what this special purchase was. The coffee mugs were filled and washed again and again as by dinnertime more than forty people had called all with the same purpose.

Bridgetown Boy paraded at various shows up and down the country and settled down to work with the milking herd. Tests were done on him to find out if he was suitable to send off to a nearby A.I. centre. Yes, he was eligible so off he went.

Our first Belgium Blue calf was due on New Year's Day, and we waited with baited breath for the new arrival. A normal birth and a bull calf of a blue and white colour was jerkily trying to stand. Alf as he was known was named after my father who originally owned the cow that borne him. Alf was not Bridgetown Boys calf but from and A.I. trial of crossbreeds before seriously starting the pedigree herd.

Bridgetown Boy's first calf, Christmas Box was given to me as a belated Christmas present. The first week he was learning to walk on the halter and just handled and groomed as once learnt was never forgotten, and so much easier to do on a small animal than trying to hang onto one at say six months old. Alf ran with the cows as did the next few that had beef calves. This was the start of the suckler herd.

To promote the breed as a good cross with the dairy cow, Alf went to local shows. He loved it, maybe he understood the compliments but certainly he enjoyed all the rubbing and pats he received. When out in the field and he heard the lorry start, possibly going to market, Alf would race to the gate as he loved going off, but if the lorry passed by his bawling lasted for some long time.

Alf's confirmation was good and the Chelford September sale was looming and John thought of selling Alf as he would be a good purchase to anyone showing at Christmas fatstock shows later in the year. Well I have little influence in the management of the farm, but there was no way I was going to let someone else show Alf at Christmas when we had done the work and they would only have him for a few weeks. Many discussions took place on the subject and we agreed that John would take him to show him but not sell him and we would show him at a fatstock show. John and a friend set off with Alf and they were instructed if Alf didn't come back John needn't either, jokingly of course, but I really felt too much had been done with Alf to let him go now he was nearly at his prime. He did well at the show with a third prize which, when you think it's a national show, but imagine the friend's panic as he saw a market attendant leading Alf towards the sale ring, a route he didn't complete thankfully. Returned both John and Alf and were welcomed home.

Care was given to his diet so that he would be at his best for December. Several days before the show, Alf got shampooed, his feet trimmed and generally poshed up. The lorry starts and Alf hops up in and off to go to his last show. How I longed to go to see him do his best in the show, which had been my main aim all along. It was a long day as I waited for John to return with the result, even though this time Alf wouldn't be coming home. Proudly we had a first prize rosette to put with his yellow one from Chelford.

Christmas Box went through the same learning process as Alf, but not to the shows as by now we had more pedigree cattle, and John and Kevin took them to shows to compete and discuss other people's herds and promote the breed. Two bulls were bred here by caesarean to recipient cows, that is a cow of any breed capable of carrying the calf of pedigree parents. A lot of this was done nationally with most breeds but it was one of the first in our area. One white calf, and a blue and white one with names that had to start with the letter E. Earl and Escort were the new show cattle. Earl stayed here and we still have his descendents. I had hoped to raise Christmas Box the same as Alf but he was considered not to be quite good enough for the fatstock show so he went to market the week before so we never knew what chance if any he had.

Christmas Box, having learnt to lead on the halter, was led into the house one day as my mother wanted to see him but with both legs in plaster she was unable to get to him. He behaved impeccably in these unknown surroundings.

Giving up milking

Again John was so suddenly taken ill and a doctor called and injected him and that was John gone into slumberland for the greatest part of twenty-four hours. Inner ear problem which makes one feel as if you were on a very bad sea crossing, and as John said, the day after a good night at the pub. This took three weeks to subside. I have never had it but having watched John trying to get his balance, I don't want to either.

It was while getting over one of these bad bouts of this that he came out with his bombshell. He thought if his health was going to keep letting him down, and Kevin and I had to keep covering his work, it would be a good idea to sell the milking herd. Well, the words didn't go into my head, but I remember thinking he must be more ill than I thought.

He had costed a new milking machine because the present one had been in use for years. Restrictions from the ministry dictated up-grading yet again both milking parlours and dirty water systems. Quotas were just being enforced so all in all he thought it was a time for change. The words just buzzed around in my head as I went out with the dogs for one of the longest walks they possibly ever had. At least they were able to settle down when we did get home, which is more than I could as I just hoped that was the last I ever heard of that conversation. I agree quotas were out against any way the farmer normally worked.

The bonus had always been to work and try to improve on the previous year, but when politics get involved the logic goes out of the job. To be penalised for producing more than the amount allotted to you during a year and then import milk whilst our surplus had to be thrown away takes some understanding but then not being an academic, perhaps accounts for it. Although if questions were asked the ministry didn't know the answers so there was little hope of ever understanding their view.

John pursued his thought of dispersing the milking herd and with auctioneers the date was agreed. As previously mentioned there is always a favourite or two, and in my case there were two so the ultimatum was put forward, me or the cows went. That was no difficult choice for John as he said he would get more for the cows! Seriously it seemed sense to keep a couple for milk for our own use as having always had milk on hand I had no idea what we used in a day and in any case I had to keep my sanity.

The day loomed and although helping with the preparations, I inwardly hoped it would never take place, but the auctioneer arrived and stuck the lot numbers on each one. It wasn't that I thought John was wrong, financially he was right as it would take years to cover the costs of the imposed expenditure, and we didn't have time on our side.

Even to dwindle the herd down over the years by not replacing the old cattle that go from the herd, the upgrading of the milking parlour would still have to go ahead, which spending that amount of money was ridiculous. The parlour and dairy were all up to the milk marketing standard and the milk was the top standard so it didn't make sense at all to do all the so called improvements.

The sale day was so unusual to the cows as they would normally be out in the fields, then all the prospective buyers milling around them poking and prodding. The bawling was a noise I will never forget listening to from the house. The day over and financially the sale was successful but we were only left with the pedigree Belgium Blues and a few suckler cows. My two were milked twice daily but that only took minutes whereas it had been three hours a day given to milking. The nights were light until late and there was no way I could stay indoors so walked aimlessly until dark. It was a way of life that stopped overnight and I had never expected it to leave such emptiness.

John was kept busy with the contract work so being away from the farm probably helped him, and Kevin didn't actually milk but was involved with the care of the cows. However, John started buying in young calves to rear for the beef market. He knew the basics of this type of farming, but with so many breeds they all develop differently, so with a mixed bunch it meant some would be fit earlier and also he wanted to see good grading results.

The Belgium Blues were the ones in demand and suited our farming way. With their kindly temperament and a faster maturing rate that was the breed for us to expand with. It was very different to juggle the funds for the first year because the milk cheque was paid every month but with the outlay for the calves there was no cheque until the first ones were ready to go which takes about two to two and a half years. Once into the system it was all right again. With the two milking cows I got the cream from the milk, and what we didn't use I made into butter, so nothing was wasted and we hadn't had cream for years as we couldn't take the cream of when selling milk. It was the plan to try and get the two cows to calve six months apart so that we were not with a glut of milk or without at another time, but nature being what it is my plans went right out of the window, although we never had a time without milk.

Earl and Escort now grown up and did their turn at shows but now it was time for them to work. Escort went off to a farm up the country somewhere but Earl stayed with the suckler herd. Normally bulls with cows are best not taken much notice of because you should never trust one, but Earl would wander up and want to be made a fuss of. The sheer size gives the wrong image of the breed because they are so very quiet and love a lot of fuss made of them.

The pedigree herd was gradually increasing and with the purchase of one cow we had a lot of laughs. She was a long big cow and she knew how to charm anyone but it was the way she used to sit like a dog in the fields. Many a passer by would call in to say one of our cows maybe ill as it was sat in a strange position.

All her offspring inherited this so it still goes on. All the young calves were halter led at an early age and any showing good potential noted. A show beast would have to walk through the range of obstacles that they would come up against at a show field. Bits of cloths on poles were makeshift flags, radios were in place of microphones, balloons and of course the dogs and pony played their part. Rarely did we have any take any notice of any of these things and at the shows it was all old hat so thankfully they behaved well even if they didn't show well.

John rarely came home without rosettes and prize cards and it was good for business if the cattle were of good confirmation. He now had two ambitions; one was to get a championship at Chelford and another at the Royal Show, which is one of the top national shows. So far he had nothing of that outstanding quality but it gave him something to work towards. Bridgetown Boy came back home and for short spells went out on hire to other herds, not something we like doing but he was too good to idle his days away.

We had many phone calls asking advice as to whether to have calves from him as being so big farmers were cautious because of difficult births, but the calves are small born and then just grow at a fantastic rate. One very excited farmer phoned us after using the A.I. and one of his dairy cows had given birth to triplets. We set off to see them straight away and he had every cause to be excited, they were well matched and of good size. A delight to see, twins occur fairly often but triplets are much more rare.

The cow that would sit up produced a really good bull calf but for some unknown reason he would not suck his mother so we milked her and he would drink it from a bucket. He was born the day of the outbreak of the Falklands war and each year there is an initial letter all registered animals must start with and that year it was "I" so he was Invader. He grew into a lovely bull and he too went to shows as a calf until maturity and also went to the A.I. centre.

Not all calves were so successful one bull was small born and became so muscular but didn't grow very big at all. The prettiest marked, and lovely in every way, but with his short legs it was doubtful he would ever be able to work. At three weeks he went to a fun show just for children to play with but he wasn't good enough for shows in general. The buyer of the beef cattle took one took at him and said £1.70 a kilo for him but it fell on deaf ears, John didn't know what to do with him but running with my two milking cows Guardsman proved his little legs were no problem. With his first cow in calf he was in demand and was hired out and anyone that had him was reluctant to return him, as he was such a charmer. His calves didn't inherit his little legs so he had a good life with his females.

The vet had to visit as Guardsman had a problem with one foot. In the yard the vet was ready to look at him and was waiting for us to get Guardsman housed but we said he would be all right there. We did get a bale or straw to rest his foot on while it was being attended too, as it gets heavy to hold up.

The vet couldn't believe he had treated a bull in an open yard, he said that he hadn't even done the same to a cow before. Guardsman's little legs did eventually become his downfall. When he was eight years old the wear and tear had taken its toll and sadly it was considered kinder to have him put down than let him suffer. I fed him and gave him one last cuddle and cowardly went shopping so that the last memory was a pleasant one.

Because the Belgium Blue herd were shown, so much time was spent with them shampooing and leading, they knew exactly what we expected of them and of course we got very attached to them, but like all animals their life span is short compared to ours so many heartfelt days are spent when they have to go. The day dawned when Bridgetown Boy had reached the end of his career and our usual cattle buyer made the arrangements to take him. John bravely made the decision but was busy with contract work the day he was collected, and I was thankful in many ways he had been spared the final farewell, but at the same time to halter him and lead him into the lorry wasn't too pleasant for me, but Bridgetown Boy thought he was just going to another show so went quite happily.

Perhaps we make life hard for ourselves by getting so involved with the animals but we try to make their lives happy and they respond to that and over the years one can't help becoming attached to them. There are always new ones to work with so the time is taken up with their welfare so one can't brood too long about an old one that has left the herd.

Bridgetown Boy

Aging Dogs

One morning getting up as usual we found that Kim wasn't able to walk, which was very distressing to her and us. We left her at night appearing healthy so it was a shock to find her in this state. She was twelve years old and the expected life of a Dalmatian is eight. No-one put into words their thoughts but we were all thinking the worst. I managed to get Kim propped up against my leg and as I moved forward she moved with me. After several sessions of this during the day she became stronger. It was a stroke that had caused the problem but after about three days she was mobile on her own again.

She gained strength and it wasn't long before she and Forager were doing all the walks and playing as normal. She actually had two more strokes in the next two years but she overcame them. Forager was most concerned when she was unwell and would lie with her and lick her, which he never did at any other time. Once over the strokes she didn't lose her enthusiasm for walks, apart from being rather thin she neither looked nor acted her age. She had a good appetite but with age she got so thin, but she was happy and could bound all up the hill with the greatest of ease, which rather belied her appearance.

Dalmatians have a very shorthaired coat and because of her thinness my Mother knitted her a dog jacket. This she wore quite proudly and as we live in a very exposed area, and it's seldom warm, she did benefit. Forager thought he should have one but he wasn't to be pampered, but he was often to be seen curled up on it if Kim wasn't wearing it!

One day when he was trying to attract our attention and have this or his own jacket, just for fun Kevin put a very small woolly hat on his head and he thought that was even better than the coat! He wore it readily until at last we even found it acceptable.

Forager had the most wonderful eyes, he could charm you or scold you and I am sure he called me a lot of unrepeatable things judging from his expression. Mealtimes he was always alert in case a small titbit might be left and we realised as plates became emptier the moaning would get louder.

One day as I nearly finished my meal I told him he could have a morsel of meat if he said please. A very throaty quiet bark was the response so he always said, 'please' from there on, on request. He wasn't a greedy dog but the cat's food on the shelf did smell good to him sometimes.

Idling by the shelf on one occasion I kept busy and watched as he put his front paws on the side of the bowl and edged it towards himself. When nearly on the edge he put both front feet on the shelf and pushed backwards, gripping the dish in his teeth, lowering it to the floor without any spillage then he would eat what might be left. Once having done this it became a daily ritual. He would give us an artful look first and we knew what he was going to do.

With Kim's ageing and Forager's hunting instincts pushed to the background, and at least he liked a little chase but would come when called, meant they both enjoyed their runs in the fields. Kim now fifteen years old we knew everyday was precious, but on odd days she started passing drops of blood. The dread of loosing her loomed but was told it was a kidney weakness but until it became much worse it wouldn't affect her too much, which was the case.

Several months passed but one morning the blood was continuous so the vet was called. The wait seemed hours, as she pitifully wouldn't leave me as if I had a magic answer to what was happening to her. The prognosis was that the kidneys had completely failed and she could only have a couple of unpleasant days left or we could relieve her of that ordeal by putting her to sleep. We all knew she wasn't going to be put through suffering to gain her peace. The decision made the vet tactfully went to his car giving us a few moments with her. Lying in her chair as the vet moved between her and me she growled, even protecting me at that time. She literally died instantly and as if Forager knew he did a howl like no other I had heard before or since. We had nearly twice the expected life span from her but felt there would never be anything else that could take her place.

Certainly it wouldn't be fair to get another Dalmatian, as it would always be compared with Kim. Forager liked the undivided attention he was getting but he would race off into the fields as if he hoped that was where he would find Kim. Little did we know that Kim's replacement was born two days before she had died.

Knowing my weakness for Great Danes John read an advertisement about a litter of pups in the next village. I tried to be firm by saying we never meant to have two dogs and it was only because of Forager's misfortune that we had had two. It was decided we would go and see them, which of course was fatal, and all that had been said about we didn't have to have one but we could make enquiries, were forgotten. There were four pups only two weeks old.

We weren't expecting them to be so young and I was all for waiting to see them in a month's time. The vendor wasn't going to be messed about like that, and possibly miss out on them all being sold.

John was saying decide now and we shall know what we are doing. We didn't want the dog, and one bitch was of show potential so the price of that one and the past experience of dog shows, didn't interest me. It should have been easy to choose from two and probably would have been had they been older. One had white toes, which is not acceptable in the Dane world, but she had a lovely muzzle, which looked rather like tribal markings. Her toes didn't bother us and the more we mentioned them the price kept dropping, and as this pup lay in the palm of my hand its future was being secured with us.

Of course we had to leave it with mum for several more weeks but were invited to visit her at anytime. Restraint was exercised until it broke loose and three weeks later we took up the invitation. I sat on the floor where all the pups were asleep, but one woke up and strolled over and climbed onto my lap and settled to sleep again. Imagine my delight to discover that this little pup was the one that we had previously purchased. Her face had three dark lines going along her nose and cheeks and she looked like a Zulu warrior. I suggested Zulu would be a good name for her but no one agreed, but none could think of anything else so Zulu she was.

It was a long wait as the weeks went by until we could collect her but eventually the phone call came to say she was ready. John and I went for her to be greeted by one huge Great Dane, which was her father. He stood shoulder high to us. Mum was shut away this time as we were taking one of her pups. Complete with blanket and pup on my lap, and a list of instructions and diet, we set off home. The dog, her father, had a good sniff of the blanket and us so Zulu had a

Forager and Zulu - the same size!

few familiar smells daubed on us.

Kevin didn't go with us as he was sure Forager wouldn't like a new puppy around having had sole attention. Even we hadn't realised he had missed Kim so much until we put Zulu down and promptly Forager took her around the house and tried playing with her. They were both the same size at that time but Zulu's feet were enormous. We knew what we were taking on but the diet sheet was an accurate guideline, whilst she was growing the amount of food was increased at a phenomenal rate if bone and development were to be strong.

That first night I settled her down by the Aga on the same blanket she had travelled home on, and put Forager in another room. Expecting a few cries during the night we slept with one ear open, unnecessarily as it turned out. We were greeted in the morning with a lot of bounding about from both dogs and we were delighted that there were no puddles.

Forager followed Kim's example by schooling Zulu. He was put on the lead then Zulu and off we went. It is so easy to have one that knows what to do than have a puppy on its own. She soon learnt her name and came when called, so that meant in the fields they could run loose. As she grew, and her pace became faster than Forager's, she would do a circle at her speed before trotting along with him at his rate.

Great Danes don't need a lot of exercise, and it is not advisable for hard running whilst growing, so it was good that she had Forager to keep her under control. She just had to be with me and followed me most of the day or if asleep an eye would open to check I was still around. The amount of food she was eating was building up week by week. Tripe, biscuit, eggs and milk with vitamins but at fifteen months she started to leave some of her feed so we knew she had finished growing. She actually ate no more than Forager from then on. Now full sized people were very wary of her when they called and persistent reps decreased in number rapidly, thankfully.

The cats watched as Zulu grew and grew but were quite undaunted by her size. Ginge always was able to take care of herself with an outstretched paw but Tinker would normally choose to curl up with Zulu when indoors. She wasn't big for the breed but for a big dog she was unbelievably gentle.

One of their mannerisms is to put your wrist in their mouth and walk with you. As

Whose going to put a stick on?

the mouth opens and your arm is encased, you wait for the pain, but apart from the warmth on the arm, there is no pressure whatsoever. Friends who called on a regular basis were treated to this way of being walked with the dog and found it bewildering as they were led into me. She would not even allow these same friends into the house if we weren't in, only into the garden or on the farm. The comments were that she wasn't aggressive at all but stood across the doorway and barred them from entering. Once they knew we were outside Zulu would probably lead them to where we were.

She was a very quiet dog and always liked us to be together, but not touching one another, and would barge between us to separate the two. The romps with Forager became more boisterous as she was full size, but Forager was always able to dart under something where it was impossible for Zulu to get to. In the open he would pop in under her and she was unable to do a thing about it but she knew he had had enough rough play and it would be resumed at a compatible pace.

We had only had Zulu a few months when one of Kevin's pals phoned us. Kevin had become interested in greyhound racing and this friend had a greyhound with a damaged wrist, which would mend and should cause him no more trouble as a pet, but his racing days were over.

Greyhounds

Kevin was at his pal's when the telephone call was made to clear it with me, as with him away working I would have to be involved with the dogs welfare. There was no way we could have him in the house, and in any case he had to take life quietly if his leg was to repair.

Yet another disused pig sty was hurriedly reconstructed into a kennel. The inside had a raised sleeping area the outside area was enclosed with walls and wire. Bosun occupied the adjoining house. Mickey arrived, a beautiful black dog with white throat and paws. He was very friendly and one couldn't help loving him. He brought some of his food with him so that his diet wasn't changed all at once. A Greyhound's weight is very important when racing; they seem able to gain extra ounces overnight. His breakfast ready he was to go out for his walk, which had to be limited until he became stronger.

Kevin had to leave early that morning, so adhering to all the instructions, we set off together, and with so many new smells and things to see it took Mickey a while with little walking done. The kennel was washed and food eaten then he had well-earned rest with his friend Snoopy. Snoopy was a soft toy that he was given on race nights if he was left in kennels when other dogs went racing. He would curl up with it and stay quiet, whereas before he used to howl until the rest returned.

Racing is their one love and they are always at the ready, hence the reason they are kept on the lead. Their eyesight is very acute and rabbits could be spotted four fields away. Now that Mickey wasn't racing he didn't have to be kept to a rigid routine, he would come with me to feed the calves and soon learnt there was always a drop of milk left in the bucket, and would give me a quizzical look and lick the bucket clean.

It was John's idea that if we had one non-racing greyhound to care for why not have a racer. Another greyhound owner was going away and asked if we could kennel his three dogs. One was a particularly appealing with grey, white and brindle colouring. They settled in well overnight and were shut in the inside part of the kennel, so next morning we didn't expect them to be looking at us from the outside pen. They had chewed the door down to shreds so that they could observe the new surroundings. We hastily repaired it for the next night so they didn't repeat the previous night's caper.

It was not long before Huzz, the one I liked when they stayed, was here for Kevin to race. He wasn't the most brilliant racer and his age wasn't going to help him improve, but by having him it taught us what had to be done for a racing dog. He did win the odd race though.

On the morning of one Christmas Eve, the racing was held and Kevin set off with Huzz and returned having won his race. Kevin could only laugh when he got to the kennel where he found paper chains and little socks being ready for Father Christmas. The next morning the socks were filled and a card was waiting for Kevin.

Needless to say I was the culprit, and whilst John quietly arrived he didn't know, until he fed his pedigrees, that all the dogs had name plates above their separate pens, plus paper chains. Mickey and Huzz became good pals but it is not wise to put two dogs or bitches together, though generally a dog and bitch will be quite happy together. Their kennels were adjoining separated by wire mesh so that they could see each other.

Huzz's previous owner had asked Kevin to go to Ireland with him to see grey-hounds and some top grade racing, totally different from the local flapping track we supported. This was arranged but in the meantime yet another greyhound owner had asked us to look after his dogs overnight and it coincided with the day that Kevin was to leave for Ireland. With two extra dogs it should not be any trouble overnight, but with a dense fog that lasted all day, it meant Kevin's early morning flight was divert-ed and the owner of the two extra dogs was advised not to make the journey in such conditions and the dogs would be

Kevin with Micky and Huzz - the first greyhounds

fine.

Taking the dogs out was of some concern as the visibility was virtually nil and I knew if a fox or rabbit was also wandering, we wouldn't have any warning, and with the speed that greyhounds take off I would have no control. We set off with me talking and singing hoping any animal would be ready to run from our path. This apparently worked as exercise was done without incident. The fog lasted for a week and the owner of the two dogs phoned daily and was prepared to try the journey, but it seemed pointless to travel when it wasn't necessary. They were a lovely pair of dogs and the bitch was his pet for many years after her racing career was over.

Somehow on Kevin's return from Ireland it was no surprise that he was to be followed by two greyhound saplings, (that is young greyhounds) trained and ready to race. He had bought them from a couple who had bred and trained them themselves with the help of a friend who turned out to be a top trainer in Ireland. The tennis court, which wasn't being used as such, had a box van container placed in it. This was insulated, and a raised bed area and lighting installed making a very suitable kennel and exercise area for the two new arrivals. They were transported by ferry in a specially adapted van with individual kennel space, with a person who does this as his job. Delivered, they were led round their new surrounding to know the boundaries, this is very important as the speed they travel at, accidents can happen if they don't know where they are. They were two bitches, their pet names being Blacky and Bluey depicting their colouring. Blacky was very affectionate and so was Bluey in her own way, but she always had to be on the move and independent.

Once settled and over the journey, the time came for them to go to the track for their trial runs. This is a run done over a certain distance and timed to get the grading before they can race. They are weighed before each run and have to have two trials before they can race. Should they race over the limits allowed the race is void, once having the grading there is a level of improvement, but beyond that there could be a dubious reason for extra gained speed.

Blacky proved to be the better of the two. Bluey was well able to do it but sometimes she just appeared to enjoy a run rather than a race, which was annoying when she was capable of better, but she was an independent dog and that was that. Kevin busy with baling asked me to take Blacky one night to the track, and a friend would take her out for her race. I hadn't seen her race before so it was with baited breath as the traps opened to see which dog got away first. It was Blacky, and she led all the way and won. I was thrilled and my previous self consciousness of treading on a rather male dominated track left me as all Kevin's friends were saying well done Mother, and that's what I was known as from then on.

To return home I went via my parents and called to tell them of all the excitement. Blacky resting in the back of the car was wagging her tail furiously, with a bright eye shining with pride as she was told what a good girl she had been. Kevin had kept in touch with the breeders and sent photos of the dogs in their new terrain, so of course when he finished work that night they had a late phone call to relay his success. This phone call was followed on a regular basis.

It was when Kevin was in hospital for an operation on his knee that I first spoke to this couple, when they phoned to enquire of Kevin. Immediately we were chatting like old friends, and a new friendship was started. Blacky and Bluey had been here a few months when our Irish friends came to stay. The dogs were overjoyed to see their familiar faces and hear their accents. We all enjoyed their company and shared many laughs. Between work we showed them the local sights, and of course racing was a must with the two dogs entered. We had worked with them to get them super fit to put on a good performance, but as always when you want something to be special it never comes off. Blacky missed the get away and gained pace to end second, and Bluey enjoyed the run then started to race on the last straight, which was too late to do more than third place. With their knowledge of racing our friends knew why they were placed as they were.

A few more days and it was time for our friends to depart. The husband was terrified of flying and had refused to visit relatives in England on many occasions, so we were privileged that Blacky and Bluey had made him visit us. It seemed that we had ages before the final farewells, but all too quickly we had tears flowing as they disappeared into the departure lounge. The phone calls become much more frequent from then on, and we shared our joys and our sorrows, unbelievable that we had only known them for such little time. Huzz still had been racing but his age was against him and his legs were weakening, so he was a retired companion for Mickey.

When racing they have to be kept to a rigid routine for best results, that doesn't mean we don't have some fun and play and make a fuss of them, but they need their energy on the track not wasted at home.

Shutting them in their kennels at night had become my job. This was a pleasure, as Huzz would play bo-peep with his front paw, covering his eyes and slowly sliding it away to reveal an eye, so this was his game before a biscuit and lights out. Mickey would lie on his back and peddle his legs then smother me in kisses before his biscuits. Blacky and Bluey shared a kennel, as they had never been parted, so that is why these two bitches stayed as a pair. Sat on their bed, one under each arm, they would cuddle up and more kisses came my way. Forager and Zulu saw the greyhounds but didn't actually go out with them, as they ran freely and the greyhounds were kept on leads. It would have been too damaging to their legs in the fields to run freely, also the risk of wildlife popping up would have completely used up the energy reserved for racing.

Mickey and Huzz went for exercise with the two bitches when Kevin took them out in the mornings, and I scrubbed the kennels. That was purely to keep them fresh as greyhounds, in spite of being kennelled, are clean by nature. Kevin was able to take all out at once, but for the afternoon walks I usually did two at a time. The power they have would have pulled me over should they see something that looked like wanting to be chased. It was time consuming, but most enjoyable. Mickey's calf milk bucket would be waiting on the return from his morning walk and it was as if the others knew this was special to him as not one other went to the bucket, but patiently waited for Mickey to finish the contents, licking his lips, then they all moved on to the kennels.

Kevin visited Ireland to stay with our friends, and went to some of the top tracks to watch the racing. He learnt a lot more about racing from one of their trainer friends. He brought back photographs of Blacky and Bluey's previous home, which helped us overcome their wailing during the nights.

Shut in at night it was unusual to hear from them until morning, but since having Blacky and Bluey I would get up possibly three or four times a night to quieten them. Seeing the photographs I realised they had never known it dark, as with motorway lights at the end of the garden, it lit the premises. The solution was to leave the kennel lights switched on, and then we and they had a good night's sleep.

I have always done dressmaking, but Kevin's request for dog jackets was new to me. A local material shop was helpful in supplying a lightweight waterproof lined material. Some hasty calculations, enough hopefully of blue and red, was purchased complete with matching braid for edging and ties. With winter weather and rain approaching, two dogs blue jackets and the bitches red ones were at the ready, and they seemed quite happy as they set off one wet morning with this protection against the rain. Suddenly there was a demand for these jackets once seen at the track, so I was kept busy and the shopkeeper was having to re-order various colours to satisfy the everlasting need.

The routine of the kennel work was quite time consuming, as the food had to be soaked, meat cooked and gravy made, but for four it took a little longer than for one. It didn't end there though as Zorr arrived, a huge brindle dog. He had been racing at one of the big tracks but the trainer decided he would be worth trying on a flapping track. I don't like brindle colouring no matter what breed of dog, but the personality of this dog overcame him being brindle.

He was a big strong dog and put both Kevin and John to the ground with the power of an unexpected surge forward. Somehow he seemed to know I had to be 'handled' with care, and I could feel his shoulder on my leg as we walked and he never once pulled me. It was a relief that he treated me properly as I didn't know how Kevin would have been, or perhaps it was because I knew how he would react, if I had to tell him I had lost my grip and Zorr was last seen heading that way!

He filled up our little car if I took him racing but his enthusiasm on the track was a bit over the top as he wasn't content to win the race but had to deal with the hare, this being a wire frame covered with fur fabric. The ears were the first to be removed, which wasn't too drastic, it was when the hare was removed from the runners and the next race was delayed whilst a hasty repair was done, did it become embarrassing. His racing ability wasn't to be denied, he gave us a lot of pleasure and repaid Kevin by earning his keep.

Various other dogs of Kevin's track associates would leave dogs here if they were going away, or for some other reason, which was alright as by now all the pigsties had been transformed into kennels. Some were alright others brought their problems, such as one who would growl at me and would grab hold of my hand as I tried to put its collar on. I think it was possibly the cattle smells on my clothes he objected to, but thankfully he was only here a short time. Another could jump an eight-foot high fence, so he had to be walked, as there was no chance of keeping him in the grass pens made for exercise.

I didn't like so many dogs as for me it was non stop walking and feeding every afternoon, six pm in the evening is not my best time of day, so being tired from all the walks only to hear Kevin on the radio link from his tractor to home asking where I was and saying he had been trying to tell me to get a part as his machine had broken down wasn't his best move. As the night goes on the later the better for me but not the early evenings, no matter whether it's a good day or not.

John by now had become interested in the dogs and the Irish trainer sent over a fawn dog which was called Danny, and that was John's. A very nervous dog, who had endured some mishap at sometime as half an ear was missing. We suspected he had been mishandled as he mistrusted humans. I sat on his bed with him when he arrived and it took twenty minutes before he would even look at me. Very slowly over the next few days he began to realise he was going to come to no harm, and the pleasure he gave by wagging his tail for the first time was quite memorable. As if to apologise for his previous caution, when it was bedtime he would jump on his bed, have his biscuits, and then nestle down with his head on my lap with such expressive eyes speaking volumes. With this new found security and trust he repaid us with his racing and was putting everything he had into it, winning and being upgraded to higher standard races.

We use shredded paper as bedding which is unbelievably warm but there must have been a staple left in a piece which pierced Danny's paw. He was off racing, and armed with tweezers and antiseptic we tried to relieve him of his pain. It being the first time we had to do anything that might be unpleasant for him, I was afraid he might revert to his old mistrust, but it was a needless thought. He put his head and paw on my lap to do as I thought best and the staple was removed from a very angry looking foot. Soaked and clean, the antiseptic applied he was soon asleep. This was repeated night and morning for several days before it began to heal and gradually improved enough to get fit again for racing.

Zorr was in the next kennel to Danny and when his paw was being treated, big softy Zorr would watch whimpering as if he was feeling the pain he thought it must be causing, and was very pleased when it was all over. On one occasion Kevin went to Danny's kennel but whatever happened was so fast as Danny got past Kevin as the kennel door opened. Hearing Kevin's frantic calling, I just caught sight of Danny disappearing along the farm track with hens scattering in all directions. One didn't make the right decision another was saved by the appearance of a cat leaping towards the safety of straw bales. Luckily Danny stopped by a wire fence having passed machinery but was unscathed.

He was pleased with his efforts, after all that's what racing is all about, but not in the farmyard. We were just so thankful he was unharmed; he went back to his kennel a little bewildered why he hadn't been praised for a good run. The experience was never repeated by any of the dogs. The cats seemed to know they were best out of the way when exercise times loomed, it would be exactly a quarter to four in the afternoon when they came indoors. We could tell the time by them. Just occasionally Ginge would be missing, but as if taunting them she would be found sat in the gateway opposite the kennels. Little did she know she would need a bit more than bravery to survive if she were to remain there.

The trainer that sent Danny to us came to stay, so of course we all set off with Danny to the races. We had told him how fit Danny was, and seeing what other dogs were like in his race he should win. One can never be sure but just by knowing the dogs, short of mishap you can be a fair judge. Off this friend went to place his bet but seeing another punter put a hefty wager on another dog, he did the same. Trap opened and out came the dogs, and up the last straight Danny showed them all how it should be done. When we asked our friend how he had he done with his bet, a very quiet reply gave us the information of the change and he had lost. Of course he had to take some ribbing for that. The next week duty bound he backed Danny while we confused him with remarks like "he's put on weight so he won't run well" and "he can't win after last week's race" etc. Danny didn't let him down, and our friend recouped the previous week's loss.

We were unfortunate to have a fire in a barn containing an amount of hay and straw. This started mid afternoon and burned for two weeks. The wind took the smoke in the path of the kennels and dropped down the other side before spreading across the fields. It was impossible to exercise the dogs, as they would have inhaled too much smoke. Luckily it wasn't getting inside the kennels. The dogs were fed but still needed to go out, as their clean habits would not allow them to relieve themselves. A change of wind at eight o'clock allowed a quick dash along the farm track. They left the kennels nearly cross-legged so the relief of getting out was very welcome. We just got them back feeling much more comfortable before the wind changed yet again to the previous direction. All the cattle were in the fields, and although the farmhouse was filled with black dust, all was safe with no ill effects.

Breeding

With six night kennels full, and the tennis court used by day, I thought that was the maximum, but wrong again as Kevin had heard of an exceptional bitch that had to be retired because of wrist trouble. She was only three years old so he bought her to breed from. Anna arrived, her leg strong but not for racing. She was almost a lemon brindle she was so light coloured. She was a happy dog, always seemed to be laughing with big bright eyes. She was kennelled with Mickey and they got on well together. In the meantime, a future husband was being sought for Anna. A suitable stud dog was to be used in the north of the country when the time arrived. It was the previous owner of Mickey who was working in the area so Anna went with him and after a couple of days with the stud dog she returned to us and Mickey. Poor Mickey was quite put out that he couldn't help Anna in her hour of need but they settled down as before.

As time went by Anna was introduced to the kennel in the tennis court, where a heat lamp was fixed waiting for pups to be kept warm. This was an unknown territory to us all. Cattle calving we knew about, but for bitches and pups we didn't know the signs but just hoped Anna would. Typically after a long day's work Anna was very restless so we kept an eye on her. Kevin went to bed while I cat-napped and checked Anna every so often. One big moan was heard from the kennel, so calling Kevin we both went and sat with Anna as her first puppy was born at about midnight. Cleaned and settled with her we waited for another, but it was a long wait. We took stools out with us and had several cups of coffee while Anna appeared to sleep. Suddenly more action at last and the second pup was born at 3.30am. The first was a dog, the second a bitch - white with brindle white with dark fawn patches. A very tired Anna having washed and fed her new family settled down. Unsure that was all she was going to produce, Kevin sat with her until morning, but the two were all she had.

Greyhound puppies don't look a bit like the adult dogs, they have snub noses, which don't become

Anna

pointed until about two months. Anna was a lovely mum, so caring and careful with them and barely leaving them to see to her own needs. It was easy to name the bitch as she was born at dawn, so that was what she was called. Kevin tossed two names around for the dog but ended up with Duke.

They grew quickly and with eyes open, and none too strong legs as yet, they moved around their bed with an ever-watchful eye on them. With the warm summer a mat was put down and Anna and the pups were put outside. New smells and so much to find out they would tumble about. Anna kept their tummies full but meat was introduced and although it smelt good, they seemed somewhat apprehensive as to what to do with it, until Anna showed them with very exaggerated munching, they copied her and another lesson was learnt. They had already learnt from her that wet beds were not acceptable.

She was a super mum; she would play with them or watch them investigating some new object and discipline them. A soft collar was put on them to give them the feel, and they went back on their mat with Anna but didn't turn their heads as they sat feeling very grand and grown up. Once used to this the lead was introduced, cheating by using Anna on her lead one pup at a time to save too much tangling. There were a few hairy moments as we leapt forward and hung back but with encouragement from mum off we walked. All change the second pup's turn whilst the first one sits back with a smug expression of 'I've done that' on her face.

Dawn was becoming the more adventurous of the two; Duke would check or hang back with Anna if unsure of anything. There were walks for all three around the farm to meet the cattle and things, and then into the fields. Little legs would get tangled up, or a bottom would be seen in the air as a somersault was accom-plished, and off we go again. If play was getting out of hand a gruff bark from Anna brought them to her side until a controlled playfulness was allowed.

Duke relied on Anna's encourage-ment to try new things but Dawn was always on the go and was pre-pared for any cattle that may stand on the outside of the tennis court and peer in on them. We all had many

Duke and Duke

laughs at their antics and reactions to different things. An abundance of rabbits on the hill were of great interest to them which we thought to be a good sign

Duke and Dawn were twelve weeks old when our Irish friends and their grand-daughter visited us again. The pups were due for their first injections. The husband took Anna for a walk, whilst we set off to the vets with pups in a cardboard box for their first car ride. They took no notice of the injections, and apart from concentrating on how to destroy the box, took no interest in the journey. Reunited with Anna there was much sniffing and washing to be done.

Our friends watched Bluey and Blacky race, and this time with better results than on the previous visit. One evening I was cooking dinner for us all and my parents, so our friends took Zulu and Forager for a walk. This seemed a good idea and they knew how long they had before the meal would be ready. The deadline came and went with no sign of them returning, but suddenly the breathless granddaughter appeared to announce the dogs were lost. Off we set up the hill to see her grand-parents pacing and calling. It turned out that they sat in the shade of a tree and the dogs were with them when a fox just happened to amble their way.

Forager just couldn't resist the temptation and set off in hot pursuit, Zulu not wishing to miss out on the fun, went as well. The hill is surrounded by woods, so as the dogs disappeared they had no idea which way they had gone. Knowing the lay of the land and where the fox earths were was to my advantage but I did have visions of Forager stuck in one very big earth. It must have been a good half an hour before Forager came back, but where was Zulu. Tracing back his tracks Zulu was found behind a wire netting fence, so had to walk until there was a place for her to get to us. Two very weary dogs, and four even more weary and relieved people, returned for this somewhat now stewed meal. We all ate hungrily having found two bewildered parents settled into an unwelcoming house. It was not until next day that our friends laughed and joked about the incident, as they thought I would blast at them if any harm came to the dogs.

The biggest laugh was that the husband never eats pork, he just doesn't like it, but he had a clean plate because he thought he hadn't better get two things wrong in one night. A lot of teasing lasted for the rest of their visit. Needless to say the dogs had a good night's sleep and were pleading for a repeat treat the next day.

The four racers were all running, but the track manager and some of the owners were getting impatient with Zorr damaging the mechanical bunny, so Kevin let him go to someone who wanted him and would run him on a different track. I still didn't like his colouring but he was so gentle towards me that I didn't like to see him go, but hoped he would be happy and still enjoy his racing.

Kevin took four dogs to a track for trials one weekend with another owner and two of his dogs. An early start but it was already showings signs of being a very hot day. Leaving with plenty of water and dehydrating liquid, they thought it would be all right whatever heat would develop during the day. Somehow I was feeling uneasy about this trip, really because I felt Kevin was too tired for the track in the heat, as work had left very few hours for sleep. When the phone rang later in the afternoon I just knew it was Kevin in trouble before answering. Thankfully Kevin was all right, but Danny had done his trial and run well but while resting he became really ill.
Everyone at the track tried all ways of helping him but to no avail. Those in the know suggested his lungs had taken I too much air. On the now delayed journey home, his condition deteriorated and sadly he died. We were all very filled with our own thoughts that night as Danny had been going to spend his retirement years in the house with us.

Racing does have its accidents as greyhounds legs are so fine and the speed they travel at there is a great risk of damage if they knock something whilst moving. Somehow we prepared for that possibility, but what happened to Danny is known but far more rare, and being our first disaster, and to such a good faithful dog, seemed unjust. Contrary to many people's opinion of farmers, we are a soft lot in spite of dealing with the death of animals more frequently than people in a lot of professions. It doesn't make us unfeeling or hard.

A hasty phone call was made to our Irish trainer friend, to find a replacement for John. It took a few weeks before, what was considered a suitable dog, was sent over. It was midnight by the time he went into his kennel and we thought having been fed he would soon welcome sleep. I was just getting to bed myself when the endless howling started, so down to the kennel I march muttering non too polite things, as no one else seemed to be going to sort out why all the noise.

I sat with Shane and curled up with him and he would settle, but as soon as I made my exit and got in the house, howling resumed with crunching sounds as the door was being chewed. It was this night I found out how warm the shredded paper was, as this was how the next few hours for me was spent. By 4 am, not feeling any too pleasant by sitting up whilst a dog slept, I left to got to bed. Sleep wasn't easy as the noise of the kennel door being destroyed and the howling continued until Kevin went and sat with Shane. He was fine the next day and was busy finding out the new surroundings with interest. The next night when shut in for the night it all started again, and it dawned on us what the trouble was, he was claustrophobic. Pull the door too, but leave about an inch open peace reigned.

With a build up after his travelling, and sleepless night, he had his two trials to do to be able to start his racing. He did well and he won his first race, which was followed by many others. His panic of being shut in the traps was to his advantage, as with the desire to be free he left the trap with such thrust, he usually led at the start but sometimes cornered wide, which cost him time and sometimes races. He always raced better from spring to autumn but never so well in the colder months.

It was usual for me to take him to the track to meet Kevin and take him in parade and race and then I brought him straight home. This was done because Kevin did take once him in his car, but whilst Kevin went to get the programme and pay his entry, Shane was again in an enclosed area of the car so spent his time trying to escape by tearing the lining of the car roof. This was inspite of wearing a muzzle and all the windows being left slightly open, so it really was a big thing with him. We found out he had been reared on a farm, slept on the hay and ran around as he wanted and had never known restriction until his training began.

All the other dogs Kevin had taken with him would wait in the car for their race and rest afterwards, but with Shane it was down to me. On route to the track I would drive through the housing estate and usually people would be walking dogs, and often big fluffy cats would be wandering. Shane spotted them all and by the time we arrived he was full of go to race.

On one occasion, setting off to race I had a puncture in the car. Luckily I hadn't got as far as a long lonely road that runs through the moors, and I got back to a neighbours house and rung John to bring the pick-up so that I could resume the journey. John duly arrived but the tilt was not on the back of the pick-up, and Shane just didn't fit into the car, so we had to abandon that trip.

By now the race was nearly due so John drove home to phone Kevin and explain what was going on, as he would be wondering why we had not turned up in time to weight in. I walked Shane home with the aid of a torch along a narrow country lane with fields surrounded by woods. I just prayed the beam of the light didn't pick up the eyes of a fox or badgers, as Shane knew he was due to race and was fit and ready to go, but all was well and after the new experience of a brisk walk in the dark after normal bedtime hours he welcomed his tea and sleep.

Shane was to spend about three years here, and just about paid his keep, but his racing years ahead would be limited due to his age. A couple had wanted to buy him ever since he came here, so it was decided they could have him and being like ourselves, he was assured a good retirement when the time came. By now our kennels were full and to accommodate another retired one in the not too distant future didn't seem very practical.

Shane kept racing for some time but gradually his standard dropped and retirement came his way. Kevin saw him several times after he left us and he would be made a fuss of.

Duke and Dawn, now fourteen months old and fully developed, were ready for training. Although speed is their natural desire they have to learn what the traps are and find out if they run better on the inside or outside of the track. They were taken to the kennels. Anna had come home for the training period and it was Dawn that had good potential. Duke was bigger and slower and not going to be of the same standard but should be all right. Some dogs improve later than others, certainly with Anna's racing qualities they should do well. Returned to us, Kevin intended racing them at the local track before letting them go to a bigger track.

It was in Duke's second trial that he came off severely lame and Kevin said he didn't think he would race again. A visit to the vets, and phone calls to greyhound specialists, it was decided that an operation to pin the ligaments and bone, and plaster for six weeks had a ninety nine percent chance of complete recovery and racing could continue. After much deliberation, we decided to go ahead with the treatment, but at that time we didn't know he would have to have four more anaesthetics to set the leg in a different position every fortnight. He was so good to put up with it all but not being the boldest

Kevin with fully grown Duke and Dawn

creature, it did make him panic if he knocked himself or someone he didn't know tried to touch him. However, the day eventually came for the plaster to come off altogether and he did limp, but was expected to lose that after a few days. He did get stronger and gentle walks were introduced and then longer ones, and gradually he became fit.

Kevin eventually took him to trial for racing but his limp was worse so rested him again before the next visit to the track. The next trials and the leg just wasn't strong enough he would limp again so his career stopped before it started. His leg became strong enough to enjoy life but never to race.

His limp gone, during the warmer days he was put into the tennis court, which is where he spent his days in plaster. Immediately he was loose the leg was lifted up as he remembered why he had been there before. Even now years later he limps in the courts but nowhere else.

Dawn in the meantime had worked her way up through the grades at the local track, so Kevin was looking for a racing kennel to take her for a top grade. She moved to a kennel to be able to race at the Brighton and Hove Stadium. She qualified with a good grade, and was to have her first race in the afternoon. The distance between her and us was nearly two hundred miles and it meant Kevin couldn't be at many races, however, this race would be on TV at the turf accountants in the local town. An excited Kevin returned after the race beaming as, yes she had won it. We got the results on teletext, but of course missed the action.

She kept racing and gaining time so moved up the grades rapidly. As Anna had been an open race winner several times, we hoped maybe Dawn would follow that course. Kevin occasionally went to watch her race and was greeted with great affection as she saw him approach her. She did well at her racing but with bitches they have a twelve-week rest after they have been in season, so of course she reached her peak and had to stop for the said reason. She raced until she was nearly five years old, but her grades were slowly dropping, and with changes at the kennel, Kevin brought her back home.

The local track closed at almost the same time, so she joined the others in retirement. She paid her way and added some very nice trophies to the cabinet. As her racing covered nearly four years there were still a lot of comings and goings regarding greyhounds during that time back home.

Racing one night locally, an owner was not pleased with his dog's performance and said he would try it once more, but not being the most pleasant person, threatening that if the dog didn't do something good, not only would his racing be over, but also its life. The following week Kevin phoned from the track for me to collect a dog, you have guessed it - we now owned the poor dog that didn't please its owner. Well this pathetic creature travelled back with me and it needed feeding up and affection to become confident. A lovely dog and longed to be appreciated for what he was. Kevin gave him to me so we built him up and didn't worry about racing for a while as we suspected he had some bad memories of racing as, if anyone lifted a hand quickly for any reason, this poor animal just crouched to the ground.

Eventually a happy and fit dog, we took him for his trials, which he showed good time, so his first race for me was to follow the next week. I took him and Kevin put him into the traps and out shot Earl and steamed ahead, not anything else anywhere near to catch him. I contained my excitement as he was still leading to the last bend when to my horror he just stopped and waited for the others to catch up and ran to the finish in the middle of the bunch. We still made a fuss of him and hoped he felt good because he had shown he could run.

Of course Kevin now full of racing knowledge, told me he didn't think he would make good but undaunted, I at least now had a happy dog so that usually means they like to repay with their best efforts. Again we set off racing and again he leads and I'm sure he has got it this time, but again he waits for the others and his name was not with the placed dogs.

Several more races, in spite of all the people in the know were willing him on still had reservations he would ever do anything else as he wouldn't run without other dogs with him, and eventually I had to agree as he followed his pattern of racing. At least he had become a confident and affectionate dog that was to enjoy the rest of his days with us. Sadly he didn't have as long a time with us as we had hoped because his kidneys let him down. He didn't respond to the vet's treatment, and as he had had enough bad experiences in his early life, we decided this time we could release him from further suffering, which was his predicted future.

Kevin, Blacky and Bluey had raced on a regular programme weather permitting, but Blacky showed signs of lameness. After thorough inspection a small corn was discovered on one pad. She took the corn plaster off during the night so we were advised that a boot from a pet shop would prevent more destruction. I could have bought a cheap pair of sandals for the price asked so I inspected it well and came home and made one from soft leather. It may have lacked detail but it worked.

Bluey's racing was on the decline but Blacky's enthusiasm never waned. However, Kevin decided to let them go to another track and owner. It was not a move I ever accepted but it was nothing to do with me, they were his dogs. The day they went I sat and cuddled and cried with them, praying Kevin would see to change his mind. I can see them now everyday as I remember them going along the farm track in the back of the car. Bluey enjoying anything that filled her day so a car ride would be great, but Blacky just watched me until out of sight. As they went one way, I walked onto the hill and into the wood to give vent to my feelings. I personally could never agree to the move and desperately hope they will return to live out their lives with us. They had listened to my moans and worries and shared my joys, as it is easier to talk to animals to unleash problems as they only listen and don't advise or interfere. Blacky particularly seemed to know my moods and would move closer and her eyes said all the right things. I suspect Bluey just thought, "Oh here we go she's had a bad day" and would snuggle up but go to sleep. It was these two that got me into going racing, and following it with interest, and I doubt if anyone else knew the bond we had, even with all the dogs we ever had there were no truer ones than them.

My milking cow and calfs

Milking

Milking my two cows had been going well until one had to go because she had a problem with a knee which couldn't be cured. One cow gave sufficient milk but they gradually give less during the months they carry the next calf and need a rest for six to eight weeks before the calf is born so we were alright for a while but the time would come for a replacement. This was done easily with one of the suckler cows, that is a cow that doesn't get milked but rears her calf on the milk.

She was a cow that lost her calf at birth and she was one from the milking herd previously so she took to milking quite readily. It was only a relatively short reprieve, as she didn't get in calf again so when her milk dried up she too had to go but at least she had a year of filling the gap.

My father, now in his late seventies, and cold winter approaching, felt it was time to give up milking his Jersey cow; now ancient but still in good form. He offered her to me knowing she would get the same treatment as she had always known. The day she came to us she settled in well and in the afternoon she went straight into be milked and produced a good lot of milk, whilst eating her feed nuts at the same time. Excitedly next day I was telling my father all that she had done and he was pleased to get a good report. After the third day of her stay here she seemed like part or the family, so we were not prepared for the shock ahead.

The next day's milking was a disaster as she wouldn't eat the nuts and she had not a drop of milk, she gave no signs of being ill, and the only change to her diet was silage. We kept a close watch on her all day and at the afternoon milking time I had to get the cow in to where the machine was, but to no avail still she wouldn't eat or had any milk. This was serious as no cow just stops producing milk for no reason but she settled down with others for the night and didn't seem perturbed in anyway. The next morning she wasn't looking at all happy, and was offered different types of feed to tempt her and the vet was called.

It was the afternoon by the time he arrived and did all the normal tests, but his prognosis was dismal. As she had spent all her years, which were many, on one farm with one handler, she just couldn't accept the change. We thought it simple, just take her home, but were told the damage was done but she should be watched for any changes. Dad came to see her and that didn't cheer either him or her up at all. She wouldn't even lie down and just got weaker. Nights were broken to check the cow several times a night, and it was obvious on my last visit she was giving up. She was laid down and I sat with her and rambled on telling her she would be alright and so on, which she put up with. When you have spent a lifetime with animals you can read their thoughts through their eyes and eventually she made it quite plain for me to let her go to sleep. I went back to the house and after a coffee crept back to her to find her wish of that long last sleep had been granted. Everyone wished none of this had happened, and I had never heard of this before and just thought she would just roam out her days. She knew me so it wasn't as if she was completely in a strange world but she couldn't cope with it.

A farmer in the village where I grew up was selling his farm due to ill health and that meant his stock would be sold also. As mentioned, he too had a favourite cow, very old but dear to him. He was telling a mutual friend how, although he didn't like having to sell up, he couldn't bear to think of his pet cow going into a big herd, he would like her to go where she would be made a fuss off. The friend nominated us and we were asked to go and see the cow. We were taken into a paddock where five cows grazed and one walked straight to us and waited to be patted.

The farmer said "hello Spud me old darling" so we thought Spud was her name. He was pleased we seemed to pass her inspection so it was decided she should come to us for a month and if she didn't settle he would have to think again.

She arrived one sunny morning and went in the field with my other milker, who calmly looked up from eating, and took in her new companion between mouthfuls around the field. We laughed at four o'clock to find Spud back in the yard and waiting to be milked, as that was the time she was used to. This was not a problem and as long as she had plenty to eat, she would have stood there all day. She wasn't the most beautiful animal, but she had a most appealing manner. No one walked past her without her head being pushed under an arm to be made a fuss of. The farmer came to see her on several occasions, and both were pleased to see the other, and he was most amused to see that these two cows just roamed the fields as they wanted, yet never strayed onto the road. He thought she would be happy so a price agreed and Spud was to stay. After morning milking they seemed to sniff the air and then decided if they went from the yard to the right or left, but whichever was chosen, they worked their way back for the afternoon milking.

In due course Spud was not milked for a few weeks, awaiting the birth of her calf. Excitedly we kept a close watch on her when this event took place, only to end in disappointment as the calf was born dead. She was quite distraught as she tried to wash this lifeless being, but gradually it dawned on her it wasn't going to get up so she lost interest. Her previous owner came to see her and was pleased that at least she had no ill effects from her ordeal, but she loved having to tend to her previous calves so he was vexed for her. She settled down to the milking routine and gave milk in abundance, as the other cow was not in milk awaiting her calf, old Spud kept the supply going.

Forager was beginning to slow down a little now and walks were not so long as they had been in previous years. Zulu realizing her pal wasn't covering the ground as he had done was very understanding. She would bend over Forager and then as if she had told him not to get in her way, she would race off in big circles brushing past Forager and myself as she went by, providing we stood still she had it gauged correctly, but a move on our part and there would have been a crash. Once having got rid of the burst of energy she strolled along wherever Forager decided to go.

One day as a rabbit popped up in front of Zulu, a quick glance and an expression that seemed to say "sorry but I'm going to do it anyway", off she went and of course the speed she went, the rabbit gave in and Zulu was stood with it between her front legs and looked back to me as if to say "what's next". She never offered to harm the rabbit, and just stood aside when I called her to continue the walk. It was her gentleness that won her many friends, but she did like to join in if there was a run involved.

Forager and Zulu had many adventures and were always together but Forager now ageing, had a problem that the vet had to keep under control. He was still a very lively thirteen year old, and one late summer evening we all enjoyed a walk up on the hill with Forager running happily inspecting the rabbit burrows on the way. He ate a good supper and even wanted more, he would eat more than Zulu anyway. It was during the next day that he refused food, and wasn't taking any interest in anything. We encouraged him but got no reaction, he just wanted to sleep. Next morning he had lost a lot of condition and it was obvious this elderly old

Forager with sock

fellow had had enough.

I knew he wouldn't be coming home from the vets but at least he would get that longed for sleep. He had given all those years pleasure it wouldn't be fair to let him just deteriorate at natures' pace. Zulu ran straight to the car to greet her friend, I doubt if she was waiting just for me. Every time the car came back from a journey she ran to it just in case Forager was there. We had a china ornament; quite a large one like Forager, and Zulu would lie as close to it as was possible, obviously she felt some comfort from that. She hadn't ever known what it was to be on her own, and as if Tinker knew of her loneliness, he would curl up with her and go for walks skipping and dashing around making Zulu join in, so she didn't mourn for long though I'm sure she never forgot her real friend.

Christmas Box

More Puppies

The greyhounds were still doing quite well and if not winning when perhaps we thought they might, then at least they were still giving us a lot of pleasure. Kevin thought he might have another litter with Anna's help. With plenty of time to think about this he read of the stud dogs on offer. Their form and their offspring's form, was studied in depth to select a good racing line. This done, various studs were contacted but that wasn't so simple as some were fully booked for weeks ahead, others were way out of Kevin's price range. Mentioning his idea to our Irish trainer friend, he suggested a dog in Ireland and would make the arrangements and kennel Anna. This was put into motion but we had to wait for the right time for Anna, which wasn't expected for a while.

Kevin was going to Ireland for a few days in October but it was not a problem because Anna wouldn't be ready until later in the year. Animals and nature have a way of bending the rules, so it was a surprise that the need for Anna's journey became imminent. Hasty telephone calls to Ireland and to the dog transporter, only to find he was travelling that night and not going again during the time it was vital for Anna. Kevin loaded Anna and met the transporter for the crossing that night. Eagerly we waited for news of her arrival, which in due course we received. She was fine and quite happy and she knew our friends, which was good for her. The kennels seemed empty without Anna as she was always trying to control any misbehaviour.

Would you believe that when Anna was to return to us, was when Kevin would be in Ireland. It was arranged that she would be delivered to Bristol where someone else would be collecting dogs for himself, and pass through a town seven miles from us where I was to meet him. I was to get details of time as he left Bristol, and we were to meet in a factory car park.

It was that night that a cow decided to have a calf but there were some complications and she needed a caesarean birth. Getting to the house and making coffee for vets at a quarter to midnight, I was grateful that cow and her calf were doing well. The call comes through to fetch Anna. Off I set and parked the car in the car park and waited patiently, then not so patiently. I got out and walked along the pavement to have a look if there was a parked car anywhere. Well it turned out the factory had four car parks and we had chosen two different ones to use. Seeing a man walking a dog in the distance, and in the streetlights not quite able to see what sort of dog, I called out rather cautiously as I didn't know the person I was to meet. Hearing my voice, the dog's ears pricked and she stood trying to hear it again. On hearing her name Anna's tail wagged furiously, so we knew we had it right. She came in for a belated tea or maybe early breakfast, and the vet still here was impressed with her condition, and with lots of fuss she went to her kennel to enjoy what was left of the night to sleep. A very late call to Kevin to say she was home and tucked up in a warm bed. He hadn't actually seen her as their journeys meant as one arrived, the other was leaving. The puppies would be due the beginning of December, which would be seventeen months after Anna's first litter.

It was December 6th that John got up first and checked Anna to find her with three pups, and checked again after the other greyhounds were walked and another two were with her. After our breakfast, another visit to the kennel and Anna had her complete family of six. Four bitches and two dogs, four were white with some brindle or fawn markings, except one that was all white with the smallest coloured marking beside her eye, two others were dark brindle. Again Anna was a brilliant mother, always washing and caring for this larger family. The pre-dominately white puppy was a loner and was always curled up on her own away from the others. It was cold weather but with the aid of a heat light the kennel was warm but this one pup was never as warm as the rest, hence when I went to the kennel I would tuck her into my padded waistcoat, where she would snuggle in.

During one very cold, frosty night the temperatures had dropped below zero, and accompanied with a gale force wind, the electricity suddenly went off. With puppies only a few days old the heat lamp was vital to them. I thought of wrapping a hot water bottle in a blanket to maintain some heat, then considered it unwise in case Anna bit it and it leaked. It was three and a half hours later when lights burst into dazzling brightness, so quickly I dashed to the kennel. I hadn't accounted for Anna's maternal instincts, but was full of praise and admiration to find six young pups covered in shredded paper tucked tightly to Anna, with her legs around them to keep them together. One can only marvel at nature, and the pups were none the worse for the lack of heat.

One of the brindle pups appeared all right, but somehow there just seemed to be something about him that made me think he may not survive, but couldn't say why. This opinion proved right when one day Kevin saw Anna deliberately lay on this particular puppy.

Hastily we picked him up and blew into him to revive him, and rubbed him until

Anna and her new born pups

we considered him all right. As their eyes opened, this pup only had one eye open and later an ear became withered and came off so a visit to the vets he was left to sleep forever. Strange how the animals would deal with weaklings, they always know the survivors and losers and its only man's interference that gets it wrong.

Names had to be thought of. The one with the markings around the eye was Susie for obvious reasons. One had the most beautiful misty blue eyes, which could charm you as she showed the white of them. She was to be Misty. The brindle dog was Rusty; the other dog was Major and Sally the other bitch. Susie was the one I really lost my heart to and Kevin gave her to me to look after. It does entail a lot of time to rear a litter and he had his work, which took him away from home. They learnt to eat solid food and ventured outside into the big wide world with unsteady legs and sometimes frosty ground. What was meant to be a big leap to race off, ended up with a pile of puppy on the floor. Kevin spent that Christmas with our friends in Ireland and was instructed not to unpack one bag in the suitcase until Christmas Day. He was very surprised to open a card covered with puppy foot-prints with their names beside the appropriate paw mark. I had mixed up some soil with water in a saucer, and pressed a foot of each pup into it then onto the card, Anna also had her turn. This was done without Kevin's knowledge and I was sure he would notice each pup had one dirty paw where as all the others were pink and soft, but he didn't.

Anna would watch the antics of these little fluffy bundles and as they grew she was unable to stand back and watch any longer, and would often be the ringleader to start a good romp. It was most interesting to watch Anna. One night as I let her out for her last run before bed, there was a dog barking in the distance and as Anna bounded out followed by the pups she stopped to listen, and with a very throaty sound, stopped the pups mid-stride. They never moved while she listened and sniffed the air, and took a few steps forward then waited again; still unsure it was safe to let the pups join her. Some moments later another softer sound from Anna and all the pups bounded out. She saw to her own toilet needs and each pup was checked before she would take them back to their bed, and woe betide if one had not done what was necessary.

On another occasion she wanted them all one end of the pen, but Rusty was far to involved to obey so a few demanding barks were ignored. The four pups with her had a quick glance from her, which made them understand to stay put whilst she went to Rusty and gently but firmly caught hold of his ear and led him back to the others. If only humans followed this example of discipline, perhaps it would be a better world now.

Kevin would be on the floor and would be covered with puppies jumping on him pulling his shirt and trouser legs. This was great fun, but as they got older and stronger, the shirt didn't always withstand the pulling on it. Usually I wore an anorak complete with hood, and I would kneel down with the hood pulled well over my face, and they all rushed forward to find my face. Anna always was in the thick of these games; she was just like a much bigger puppy.

A puppy pulled off my glove one day so they all had to run around with it and share it but that wasn't so exciting, but Anna had to have her turn and was tossing it into the air and chasing after it again. As you can imagine, although it is a lot of work, we also had a lot of fun.

On one occasion after one of Anna's walks, Rusty would not go back to the kennel and with the other four in it was difficult to keep them there and coax the last one in, however Anna helped. She carried her lead outside and dropped it on the floor. Of course Rusty went bounding along to pick it up, but Anna had one end and took it back to the kennel with Rusty in tow and the problem solved.

These pups were developing their individual characters now. Major was the mummy's boy, Sally the bossy one and could be quite aggressive if she thought about it. Susie still the independent one, Misty the charmer and Rusty was just matter of fact about everything. They were all very loving and biddable, but all very different.

All racers have to be tattooed, and it was a very pathetic little group that sat on the mat in the sun with green ears, which possibly were a bit sore. When Duke and Dawn had their's done, it was night time and to make sure Anna didn't lick their ears, I had them in with me. It was like watching very tired children refusing to sleep as the television fascinated them and they just had to stare at it. A little head that was beginning to droop would be jerked up quickly, and eyelids took longer to blink but they didn't give in until returned with dried ears to Anna for the night.

With long hot summer days Anna would lay outside with her family in one long line behind her. The positions were always the same. Major next to her, followed by Misty then Rusty, with Sally in front of Anna and Susie ahead again. The lead training was a bit of a nightmare as four were shut in whilst Anna and one pup were put through their paces. As they realised what was going on there were noises coming from the kennel. Eventually all knowing what to do, Kevin and I set off with all six dogs. Major, developing into a big dog, wouldn't go forward if Anna wasn't at his side. We alternated who walked with who to avoid them becoming just use to a too secure routine.

As they grew and were kept together, some problems did develop so for some reason, may be because of Rusty's colouring, they did pick on him, but he wasn't interested in trouble so tended to ignore them. Sally was the ringleader and eventually she did set into him, but luckily I was on the spot and was able to put a stop to it before she really damaged him, but as it was he did have a nasty tear in his skin.

Sally's need to be first out of kennel was so strong that she wasn't very polite to any of them should they lead. Being

Anna's fully grown family - Misty, Suzie, Major, Sally, Rusty and Anna

a very hot summer, a shallow large container full of water was put for them and they all loved to lie in it. For some reason other people's dogs were here besides Kevin's own, and we had sixteen here altogether. It was far too many as for me it was non stop dog work, and of course Kevin was not here to help due to the contract work.

One brindle bitch that was here was a real pain. She was very strong and wilful. If she didn't want to walk she would sit down, and nothing would move her until we gave in and headed home. On one occasion Kevin was walking some, including this brindle, and I had some others. A rabbit popped up as quick as a flash the brindle slipped her lead and was gone off in hot pursuit. Kevin handed me what he had with him, to walk back with the ones I already had, whilst he went to rescue the one that had just disappeared through a hedge. Of course the ones I had were now all on tiptoe and wanting to join in the fun, so I think most were walked backwards to the kennel. It was rather too many for me to manage but other than not wanting to leave the scene where the fun started, they were good. Kevin soon returned with a somewhat breathless but luckily unscathed dog. She did nothing during her stay to endear me to brindles. There were no tears lost when finally she returned to her home.

I don't like being responsible for other people's animals, and especially greyhounds as they are always at risk if racing. One little bitch kept falling over when racing and then when out for exercise, and a brain tumour was the problem. The owner was very good about it and knew it could have happened at his home, but it was here and we felt awful about it. Another one gashed her leg when racing and had to be stitched, but the damage was done and she couldn't or didn't stretch out, so her training ceased.

The puppies were a year old when Kevin started making enquiries for a trainer to take them on, because at fourteen months they would be ready to start. It was a trainer some miles away that was selected, not only because of his ability, but he also used our local track. When they had some knowledge of what to do, the pups plus Anna were loaded into the back of Kevin's estate car. Anna was taken to keep them in order, as she knew to lie low and would make sure they did as well. Kevin and the friend that went with him left some rather bewildered pups, but with food and new surroundings having been explored, the eyelids were not far from falling. Anna didn't make any fuss about the loss of her family and returned to the company of Mickey.

Reports came back from the trainer that they were settled, but what were they used to eating, as they didn't seem to approve of what was on offer? I had always noticed the rare feed of chicken was soon devoured, so off to his local supermarket the pups had the meal that was appreciated, and set them going on with their other feeds.

The day came when the pups were going to the track to have a run, so off Kevin went to see them go round, and every move had to be accounted for, but being a man of few words, the best report we had was "they were alright". With all back and ready to race they went off to the track. Kevin took them several times to get really used to it, and there was always a bit of family rivalry as to whether my Susie, or one of Kevin's, was the fastest. It varied from time to time, but generally they all improved and did actually start racing.

Major's main concern was to look for Kevin and run back to him, so as soon as Kevin got to the track someone else would take him over, but even that wasn't too successful, he knew Kevin was there somewhere.

Kevin thought they would do better with a trainer on another track, so he set off again with them to their new abode. I didn't really want Susie to go, only because I wanted to see her race, and because of the distance, it would be impossible. It was a long day having watched her disappear with her looking through the back window of the car. Unknown at that time, our separation wasn't to be for long. The track was too demanding, but at least it showed what each one was capable of.

Susie was steady but not particularly fast, so she came home to the local track. Rusty had been sold before the training started, and although now racing, he wasn't making much headway. It turned out that always being a big dog, which does make it more difficult to corner, but upon investigation he had an extra bone in his back and this was preventing him from cornering tightly, so he was retired and enjoyed a family home as a pet.

Major's interest in racing didn't develop, but someone watching him spotted that he would probably make a good dog for coursing. He took him and his hunch was right and his future was secured.

Sally was thought to be more suited to hurdling so she went to do that, which she could do well, clearing the hurdles with no effort, but her temperament was still that she had to be first, which wasn't always the case.

Misty kept racing but with no great improvement, it was all rather disappointing that they didn't do better as both parents had such outstanding successes. Susie being the only one back home and still racing. she was such a charmer, wherever she went people always wanted to purchase her. Kevin thought it would be quite a good idea as her racing was no great shakes. There was no chance of me parting with her, as her charm had won me over right from the start. However, when she did win her race laughingly I told one particular persistent hopeful buyer she was well out of his price range now.

No more racing

Unfortunately with changes at the track from different managers that came and went, the track gradually went down hill so we didn't take her any more. By the time Susie had finished racing we were down to six retired dogs but not for long as we were to loose Huss. Always his kennel was clean but one morning his kennel was in an awful state and he was an obviously unwell dog. During the day he bucked up and ate his food so we though he had probably picked up something undesirable and given him a tummy upset. Next day his kennel was in the same mess and Huss had just wasted away over night. Taken to the vet we had quite a shock to discover he had bowel cancer. There had been no indication of his having anything wrong with him until the previous day so we were quite unprepared for the diagnosis.

The only way of survival was to keep him on a drip with medication an idea we didn't entertain as his age was against him and how could he possibly enjoy life, he would only be kept alive. It sounds as if with all the losses of animals we are a callous bunch but it's always a very quiet household for a few days. Everyone with their own thoughts, rightly or wrongly we like to think we have spared suffering and thought of the animals feelings before our own.

It was an acquaintance of Kevin's that wanted his greyhound bitch to produce a litter, but with nowhere to carry out this, as he only lived in a flat above his work, you've guessed it, Kevin offered to have her. Kevin and the owner took her to Ireland to be mated there, and a few weeks before the birth she was to come here. She arrived, yet another brindle, why do they keep finding their way here? Never have I seen such an expressionless animal, she never altered her expression whether we played with her or not. She never wagged her tail. She was no trouble but it was a one sided effort for conversation, even when her owner visited her there was no reaction, but at least we knew she wasn't unhappy it was just her way.

Eventually the day came and it was apparent the pups were due to be born. Even this brought no delight to her, and she decided it was too much of an effort. Having left her to get on with the job in hand, and checking her at regular intervals, with no results two hours on, we phoned the vet. We were advised if she hadn't got moving in the next hour to take her to the surgery. Bundled in the back of Kevin's car an hour later, she received an injection, which should hurry up the litter of puppies quite quickly. As Kevin returned with the bitch, and the addition of one pup, we thought all would be straightforward. Wrong again, and another phone call and trip to the vets. Sometime later, yet another injection and two more pups reluctantly found their way into the world. More could be seen moving about in mum but again she was doing nothing to help with their arrival. Two more trips took her to the vets, which ended up with Kevin bringing the next injection home in case yet another was required. Eventually six pups had been born and laughingly I suggested that she had enough and not to bother with anymore injections. The vet phoned at the time arranged, and yes certainly there were more pups, so the next injection was vital. Two more pups finally completed the family but what a day, it had taken eleven hours to produce.

The pups were all healthy comprising of six bitches and two dogs. All of mixed colouring, two were blue fawns which when their eyes opened were blue, they looked very smart. One dog was very distinctive, with his black tan and white markings with a very oversized coat, so he was nothing but wrinkles. Two others were similarly marked, one being the other dog but much smaller. The others were either a deep red fawn or light fawn. We went to bed at night with the pups clean, fed and warm under a heat lamp with mum to look after them, or so we thought.

Next morning mum was showing no interest in her family, but with encouragement she did feed them, but that was all she didn't bother to clean them or cuddle them up. It was time consuming to make sure that the pups got fed, at least cuddled up together under the lamp they kept themselves warm. The bitch never took any notice of them whatsoever, and at two weeks old it was evident that some pups were not getting enough food, except for the long dog with the wrinkles, he was always getting what there was on tap. Warmed milk was carried to the kennel and seven hungry pups quickly lapped this new diet and with full tums soon flopped in a heap to resume sleeping.

Meat was introduced, and with barely open eyes they each learnt the art of eating. People in the know were throwing in comments that we wouldn't save any of them, but none of them were ailing or weak. A chance meeting with the vet, and having related the story of how mum was not

The pups the mother didn't want to know

helping with the upbringing of her brood, he seemed somewhat shocked that all pups were fine, but did advise a very expensive milk powder that was full of the right vitamins to help strengthen their growth.

Bobby the big dog refused to accept the bitch had no milk, so often he had filled up on the new milk drink and meat, would fall asleep trying to suckle for what he hoped he would find. The owner was kept in touch, and indeed had visited to see the pups progress, but was not expecting to be taking his bitch back home so soon. She showed no emotion as he went to the car that was to take her home. Anna had been such an exceptional mum and that put this one in such a bad light. The pups had never been washed or shown not to wet their beds so it was a job to keep them looking good.

The main thing was they were all developing into really smart looking youngsters. Of course as their personalities started to show through, there were two that were stealing my heart. One being Sam, which I suppose was a bit like the bitch by being unemotional, but his facial expressions were descriptive. He would seldom take part in group play, but tended to sit back and watch with either disapproval or amusement on his face. Bobby the other dog was so much bigger than the others so when he went to run off with the others there was a lot of legwork, but not much ground covered. Never once did they miss their mum and all played until they just fell to sleep.

The owner wanted four of the pups and to sell the others. His choice was the two dogs and two bitches. None of them left here until they had had their injections and ear tattoos. Two of Kevin's friends bought two bitches each. The day came for everyone to collect the various pups. Rosie the rather timid one wouldn't look at me as she was put into the car to leave, but we were pleased to hear two days later she was fine and enjoying her new surroundings.

The other two were going to kennels to be reared, but as there was no room for a couple of weeks, so instead I offered to rear them until it was time for their training. The offer was accepted so Katie a fawn with a black and white nuzzle, and Kelly a blue with deep blue eyes, stayed here.

They were two super pups, so full of fun and eager to learn and please. It was enjoyable for me as I could do a lot more with two than Anna's larger litter. Katie would have been a wonderful pet, she was so loving. Kelly too had a loving nature, but as she grew she was an obvious racer, and really couldn't wait to become old enough to get on with it.

I knew their stay here would be only a little over a year before they set off for the training school, but anyone would have to be very hard not to get attached to them. At fourteen months they went off, and after three litters it seemed very strange not to have to go out last thing at night to let pups out. It didn't actually give me any more time, as again the contract season started, and in fact it left me wondering how they fitted into the day's routine. The trainer had our telephone number as Kevin had sent his pups to him. The owner was pleased that they would start their racing at the local track.

Katie and Kelly had been gone five weeks when the trainer telephoned here one morning; he had unsuccessfully been trying to contact the owner, but remembered us. As soon as I heard his voice I knew instantly something was wrong. Both pups were on the training track, and Kelly was the slightly better of the two, but with Katie catching up she just touched Kelly, and unbalanced her and she cornered into the rails shattering her leg. The speed that greyhounds travel, and the finesse of their bones, this is a common accident. The trainer sedated Kelly immediately until he could contact the owner, which was only an hour to wait to get his approval to put her to sleep. It would have been impossible and unkind to the dog to attempt any treatment because the damage was so great. It is so sad when something like this happens but the kind decision has to be met, as a young dog doesn't want to rest and the healing takes longer, and in the majority of cases the dog would be unable to race, which is what nature intended for them.

Katie was lost without her sister, but was kennelled with a kindly old dog, which she thought a poor substitute for the first few days. I really felt for her because she was the one that was slightly timid and did rely on Kelly. However she finished her training and started racing. When I next saw her she was pleased to see me, but I felt she really never got over missing Kelly, she had lost her perkiness. Her racing was of no great standard but she did her best. I only saw her race a couple of times as I thought it was as hard for her as for me to part and go our separate ways.

Changes good and bad

Many tears have been shed when different dogs have left here, but with others a sigh of relief could have been heard. With the last of the pups gone there was no rigid routine to stick to, as the retired dogs spent hot summer days in grass pens lazing in the sun or huddled in warm beds on more unpleasant days. One is seldom allowed to feel sorry, or indeed nor should do, over any animal as there are so many awful things happening, and human suffering endured which one seldom thinks of seriously until its within the close circuit of family or friends.

We had a very thrilling time ahead as Kevin had become engaged to a lovely girl called Leah. Although brought up in a local country town, she had never had the opportunity to get to know farm animals and their welfare. It was not long before equipped with wellies and overalls; she was into feeding, mucking out and putting fresh bedding for the cattle. Usually the cattle are cautious of people unknown to them, but they all walked towards Leah and she in turn showed no fear of being surrounded by them.

With the date set for the wedding and the purchase of a bungalow, I was sitting back letting it all get sorted out, as being the bridegrooms family meant the main arrangements were made by Leah's family, although we were included and asked for our opinion. The biggest thrill was mine when Leah asked me if I could make her wedding dress. I dabble at a bit of dressmaking, and had made a few wedding dresses and bridesmaid dresses, but she had no idea how much pleasure she had given me to do it. We spend one day at a bridal shop to look at styles and, having tried a straight and full style, we knew what suited her. We both nearly fainted at one price label, and with the basic shape in mind and a rough guess at the amount of material required, there was no justification for the price being asked.

The day before the wedding a few white lies were told about last minute shopping for the supper we were to have with our friends the night of the wedding, basically true, but also a trip to the local airport to meet a friend from Ireland, which neither Kevin or Leah knew about. Sadly not the couple we originally became friendly with, the wife had died after much suffering and her husband was terrified of flying, so it was their daughter I was to meet. Asking Kevin to help unload the car, he just couldn't believe his eyes, and after a quick meal, Leah was soon included in the unsuspected surprise.

Animals still had to be seen too as normal, and with a houseful of visitors taking care of themselves with breakfast and generally trying to be helpful or just make themselves scarce. Zulu was included in the activities by wearing a bridesmaid headdress that I had worn at my brother and sister-in-law's wedding.

Leah's next surprise was to leave church in a horse drawn carriage, something she always wanted, and a local farmer did this as a hobby, so it was easy for Kevin to arrange. However, neither of them knew how they were to leave the reception, as to set the plot a farmer near the hotel offered for Kevin to put his car in a barn for safe keeping, and he would see nobody went looking for it. Kevin dutifully parked his car, but towards the end of the reception, the said farmer took the tractor and baler Kevin uses for contract work, from the adjoining barn where Kevin's car was parked, to the hotel entrance. It took the greatest part of the morning to clean the tractor and two friends that were in on the secret had bows, boots and an oil drum secured to the tractor ready for the departure. With a great roar and a blast on the horn, Kevin and Leah disappeared as they started their new life together.

During the evening they called here to meet our friends, and the calf that John had given to Leah to rear, was waiting for them with a horseshoe around her neck, the dogs had sent their good wishes on a card at the reception. Normality had taken over again but John had to bring the tractor and baler back, and still adorned in ribbons and an added quantity of confetti, he felt very self-conscious of the looks he was getting from passing traffic.

We were all brought down to earth a few months later with the start of a terrible year with the loss of animals. November started with three weeks of fog, the worse possible conditions for cattle to be housed in, as the air doesn't circulate and breathing in stale air leads to pneumonia. We had sixty three, four month old calves and they were the first to start to show signs of lung trouble. The stress of being in new surroundings and the weather was the cause of pneumonia. The vets treated them every other day but some didn't respond, and with the loss of the first two, more treatment was required, and again two days later. By now they were all looking rather sick and still the fog persisted.

In another batch of older cattle another pneumonia type virus was taking over, but more difficult to detect and treat. The first victim was found dead first thing one morning, and we thought of various causes for it but not expecting it was a highly infectious disease. It showed no signs of the animal being ill, they just fell down dead. Again the vets returned to treat this latest virus, and still trying to cure the younger ones. Every morning we got up to find one or two dead animals, and in the end we were all dreading going out because of what we would find.

Yet another virus had struck another animal in another batch, and they were all fit to sell. In total we lost fifteen animals in nearly as many days which was a huge financial loss but still the vets bill had to be paid, which by now had run into thousands, but we would no doubt have lost the lot without their treatments. We were not the only ones to suffer; it affected nearly every farm and was the worst year the vets had known for thirty years.

Already feeling defeated, and generally trying to think up some way to recoup the loss, the BSE scare started. Ironically the local market was holding a special Belgian Blue show and sale on March 20th 1996, the day that the Ministry stepped in and alarmed the public and destroyed farming. Overnight the value of cattle dropped by at least two thirds. Any animal over thirty months could not be used for human consumption, and the effect of that was that our pedigree cows, which had been fetching £1000 - £1600, were valued at £300 compensation, and the meat was burnt.

For some reason the Ministry decided the age could be judged by their teeth, which is the biggest load of rubbish as, like humans, not all children loose their first teeth at exactly the same age. We always kept calving records, so when one animal was sent for slaughter and condemned for having four broad teeth, therefore supposedly making her thirty months or older, but we knew from the records she was twenty-four months old.

As we had proof but not an official record in the eyes of Ministry men so it was to be burnt, but we managed to at least get it back for our own use. Maybe their theory was we are half mad anyway, so should we get CJD from eating this beef, no one would notice. With half the world starving and us burning perfectly good food in case there could be a minute chance of contracting CJD. To this day that theory has never been proved.

Paperwork for every animal was introduced, which isn't a bad thing but with Ministry mumbo jumbo, needless to say the forms were far from clear, and because it was new to everyone. We wasted many a phone call to ask to clarify a particular query, no one knew the answer because it hadn't been asked before. Needless to say everyone made mistakes, but according to the officials it was not allowed, even if they were notified that there was an error a hefty fine was imposed. Apparently mistakes are unacceptable but only on the farmer's part, as we have received identification papers printed upside down, the ear numbers in the reverse order and numerous other slips, but it's a computer error. Clever though computers are I can't imagine it thinking to itself "oh today I'll do farm A and B papers" all on its own.

John struggled through all these papers most nights after a days work, and it all became too much but Leah offered to do it and working with John she soon took on that burden. We didn't escape one hefty fine, which added to the loss of income and the mentioned loss of cattle with the pneumonia, it was a downhill slope we were following. We thought we must have seen the worst of it, so battled on to try and make sense of the job we knew and loved before all the restrictions.

My two milking cows were still doing a grand job, although dear old Spud was beginning to look her age, but with an abundance of milk and still happy, she kept us going, whilst the younger cow awaited the birth of her calf. One afternoon milking, the young cow was very restless so it was obvious she was ready to calve, which she did within the next hour. A healthy bull calf was soon up on its feet and looking to find where the milk was kept.

Next morning this calf had been washed by mum and fed and was showing how a few jerky leaps he could run a round the yard. Passing them at lunchtime, when seeing John said how the calf was yet again feeding. John went out only to return to say the new mum was down with milk fever, unusual to get it twenty-four hours after calving. The vet arrived to inject calcium into the vein, but that was not his main concern as the cow went down and her back legs had gone out behind her, tearing all the ligaments. If she didn't get up in a few hours then she would have to be put down. We left her with water and food, and prayed she would make an effort to get up, but sadly she didn't and couldn't do it, so the vet returned to sign the certificate and make the arrangements for her to be collected for the incinerator.

With the Ministry so busily destroying cattle, with as yet not enough incinerators, this meant it was another day before my poor cow could be out of her misery. We made sure she was eating and drinking, but can you imagine how she felt, after roaming where she wanted to, not being able to move. Bad as it was to see her go, the next obstacle had to be dealt with.

The new restriction was that bull calves had to be destroyed within seven days of their birth. We bucket fed this perfectly formed and healthy calf and watched it chase about, curious about his surroundings and so full of life, just for some official to shoot him. It's all so alien to us and so unacceptable, but facts that the general public don't seem to be aware of, or else there would be uproar, and no matter how anyone tries to make these facts known, it just never gets published.

Feeling really deflated by this time, Spud is introduced to the daughter of the cow we have just lost who will calf in a few months time. She was the third generation of that family and should be a good milker. All was looking as if the dark cloud was lifting, as the cattle all seemed well, but wrong again. It was now two months since Spud had been the only one to milk, and although she didn't get in calve again, we knew she wouldn't milk forever, but again unprepared for another disaster. Nobody actually knew how old she was, she had to be at the very least fifteen, but no matter what, she was to live out her days here whether she gave milk or not. With ageing bones and wet days, her poor legs became weak and she was beginning to have difficulty with walking. We told her previous owner how she was and asked him to see her but he declined as, with his knowledge of cattle, he knew exactly what would have to happen. We tried everything we could think of to help her to no avail and the decision had to be made to relieve her of her discomfort. If left it would become unbearable for her and us to watch.

With no milk fresh from the cow it was the first time in my life I had to even consider how much we used a day. I had only known it always to be there twice a day, as much as we wanted. Eventually the heifer calved so we looked forward to plenty of milk and cream again. John helped to milk her for the first time and the second, and several more days but she just lashed out with such force he was afraid she would really hurt us. Where we milked was fine for old trustworthy cows, but not suitable for one with all this activity. A friend offered to take her and her calf to run with his herd, and hoped with milking with others she would soon quieten down, and we would have her back. After the first month she had shown no signs of calming in fact she kicked with such force and really meant to hurt. Thankfully she didn't hurt anyone, and although she did relent a little, she was not one to be trusted. Another disappointment was she didn't give the volume of milk that her mother and grandmother did, as she never got in calf again. This resulted in me not having any milking to do, which I hated but with the mass culling of cows going on I couldn't bear to buy one, only to find it would have to be killed. I started milking at the age of five and I found it so interesting, so fifty years on it was awful and very difficult to adjust to. Surely now nothing else could go wrong, it really was a terrible year at least it could only improve.

What a dream that was to be, true we had no major animal casualties, but with the cattle paper work, mistakes had been made. Nothing too alarming as we thought, just maybe a number of a calf written down the wrong way round, and when noticed notified the Ministry office, and were assured a note would be made of the information. As all farmers got inspected by the Ministry, it was our turn. All the cattle brought in for ear tag number checks, and two were wrong as previously reported. The correct number of cattle and papers, but the inspector would not accept the numbers were incorrectly written down, in spite of the numbers being on the two offending tags, but not in the right sequence.

We were made to feel like fraudsters and were issued a hefty fine. By now the European Government was joining in by dictating and renewing the feeling of the dangers of eating beef, but exporting this beef to us with no breeding records, age control and medicine records, yet all countries having herds with BSE.

We worked furiously to try to make up the by now huge loss to our income. Very difficult to improve the income when the rest of the world are flooding the British markets and won't accept our goods. One could write a separate volume on this subject, but I will get back to happier and more pleasurable things.

Pigs

With several visits to a farm where they had a few Gloucester Old Spot sows, John would return with great enthusiasm about these pigs. I have always had a weakness for pigs. Unlike the stigma that goes with pigs, they are so clean, but do like to wallow in a nice muddy puddle. They all have different characters, which make them so interesting. It was after taking some cattle to the said farm, whilst I prepared lunch, which was waiting for Kevin and John's somewhat late return. They rang to say they were running late but they had a surprise on the lorry. Well it wasn't really, as I knew it was only a matter of time before one of the sows found its way here. Hastily the sty was bedded and the pig unloaded, she was adorable with distinct spots of rich blue colour. She twitched her snout so much she was named Tabitha. She was due to have a littler of pigs in about eight weeks, so she was let out by day to root around a paddock.

As the date became nearer for the arrival of the piglets, farrowing rails were put round the sty; this was done so that the little pigs couldn't get crushed between the sow and the walls. The obvious signs were observed and feeling her one morning had estimated it would be night time that we would have our new family. We went to a funeral during the day and on our return strange noises were heard from the sty. On inspection, Tabitha was surrounded by eight small pigs. She was very protective of her family, and made it quite apparent we weren't welcome visitors. We watched from the doorway as these newborn pigs, with eyes open and grunting with contentment as they clung to a teat and fed. As soon as they are born they

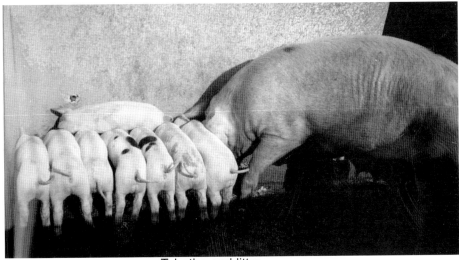
Tabatha and litter

walk straight to the teat that will be theirs as long as they need milk.

It was three days before Tabitha accepted us as she did previous to the birth of her piglets. The size of the sow compared to the little pigs one would expect them to be laid on, but watching Tabitha settle down was remarkable. She knelt on her front legs and gave a little grunt, which attracted the piglets to her head, then, very slowly, she went down on her back legs. Once settled the piglets all moved in for a feed, before falling to sleep all lined up against their Mum's tummy. Just to stand and watch animals is incredible how understanding is transmitted from one to another.

Three of the pigs were spotted the others were white. At a week old, with warm sunny days, the first trip into the outside world with Mum into the paddock. Little pigs never walk; everything has to be done at a run with a grunt as they set off. Tufts of grass sometimes meant that whilst trying to negotiate this obstacle, one got left behind so there would be many grunts as they were impatient to catch up. They would scamper around and have mock fights and tumble over and get up and race off somewhere else.

Great Danes were bred generations ago to hunt boar, and although Zulu never wanted to chase the pigs, she would spend hours watching them through the garden fence. Tabitha seemed to like Zulu, as she would come to the fence and rub her nose with Zulu's. As the summer was exceedingly hot, an old bath tub converted into a water trough was in the paddock, it was too good a chance to miss and cool on a hot body. Tabitha would climb into the bath and just lay in it, occasionally splashing the water onto her head. Her little ones got to expect this daily ritual, and would patiently wait along the outside of the bathtub.

The young pigs were eating hard food and picking up bits from the paddock, so grew very quickly. As they no longer relied on Tabitha for nourishment, they were weaned but that meant with more solid food, the cost was more and typically the market for pork had slumped. Why? because of imports yet again. So fattened and fit we put them into our deep freezer, at least we knew their

Zulu watching the pigs

history and could enjoy eating it knowing they had no illnesses or injections.

Tabitha had been to a nearby farm and met Mr. Pig. He was not a Gloucester Spot but that didn't matter, as we would only be eating what they produced. Back home again we waited and watched, as Tabitha grew fatter by the day. After eating her breakfast she went back on her bed, and about an hour later the first grunt of the first-born was heard. By the time I got to the sty it was already latched onto a teat and the second one was on the way. This time there were twelve in the litter, and as usual one was smaller than the others. After the first week it was apparent the little one was being pushed to one side and not getting its full ration, so hastily I mixed up some milk powder, then discovered I had no teat for a bottle. I carried the warm milk out in a dogs bowl and the tiny pig lapped it up readily. Two more were not getting enough and they too joined in, which was good as they all survived and grew into normal size pigs. Tabitha was less protective of this litter, she had got to know us better by now and she knew we hadn't hurt them. This litter followed the same pattern as the last, except for the three that waited for their milk.

The following litter was seven, and Tabitha was able to manage them herself. By this time the big pig farms were going out of business as there would be no financial gain by going into pigs, but we enjoy pork so weren't too bothered. It became so desperate people were taking weaned pigs to market to give away, but no one would take them. Not the best enterprise but at least we have had some laughter watching the pigs, and some super meals of home-grown pork.

Tabitha knows her name and runs as soon as she hears her name called, but the closer she is to having her piglets she starts to run with her usual gusto, not for long though as her heavy tummy nearly touches the ground. Since her first litter she has been more amiable and likes to show off her piglets to anyone that is interested. She is at present ten weeks off her next litter, so we are hoping all will go well again.

By now the two cats had died one aged sixteen and a half, the other seventeen. As usual we weren't without a replacement of a different kind. Leah's aviary had various varieties of birds, and with spring many hens were sitting, and lots of young birds to feed and pleased to see a young cockatiel leave its nest, she wasn't expecting the other older ones to pitch into it. With an empty cage since the last lovebird died, it became home to this bedraggled cockatiel. What a sight it was with no feathers on his head at all. The back and wings were also rather bare. Its appear-

John and Joey

ance certainly did nothing to endear us to it, but as usual with a creature needing nursing, we did what was required. Leah had handled it so it would sit on our hands. With the feathers so uneven over his body, flying was out for a while.

After the first week he started to get a bit fluffy around the head, which was pleasing as it was quite off putting with just skin. Feint colouring started to appear and even the tuft was starting to form. Eventually with pink cheeks and yellow head we had to admit he looked quite smart. Every night he was let out to fly, this was when Zulu disappeared into another room; she hated all the flapping rather like she did the small chicks. Listening to the bird, there was one sound that was repeated frequently and with a bit of emphasis I would say it as well. It was not too long before we were to be repaid and Joey was saying his name.

Setting the video to tape a programme, as the timing was registering it made a sort of bleep bleep sound and of course Joey picked it up. Nearly always when we go towards the television we hear this sound from the birdcage. Now with the first moult, deeper colour on the head with cream edging on the wings, at least it endorsed the fact he was male.

On his night-time flights he usually landed on John and often chewed he paper that John would be trying to read. After a while he would then come to me and I started asking him for a kiss, it wasn't long before Joey was saying it, but even more surprising he knew what to do and would nibble my lip. Time to be put back into his cage and with Joey perched on John's shoulder, John would encourage him by saying 'Joey going to be a good boy' as he crossed the room.

Usually Joey went back into the cage easily; just occasionally he would play up and fly off at the last moment, hence the encouragement. One night John had just got up to cross the room and we were both taken aback when Joey suddenly said "Joey good boy" We have had him some while now, and if he doesn't say he's good he will play up and not go into his cage, though it's rare. Obviously he gets bored with me being about the house, but if John entered the house there were excited shrieks from the birdcage. Apparently cockatiels live quite a long time, so we hope that his vocabulary remains as polite as it is at the moment. Leah has one that imitates the telephone ringing, and the neighbours are seen to stop and listen to check if their phone is ringing.

Kermit - winner of the Royal Show in 1995

A new house dog

Zulu now aged nine, which is a good age for a Great Dane, only showed her age by the greyness around her face. Her movements belied her age. One night after her meal she just blew up and was most uncomfortable, it seemed like chronic indigestion, and with a couple of tablets and rubbing her sides she seemed easier. I sat with her all night, although not quite so blown up, she was not at all well and by five thirty I did try to get an hours sleep, and I felt Zulu was going to sleep and probably not wake up. She was still not right, so we got an early visit to the vets and as soon as we walked in the surgery we were told a twisted gut was the problem.

She spent the day at the surgery on a drip in the treatment room. Everyone fell in love with her and no one would put her into a kennel, so she watched cats and dogs receive their treatment. We were able to collect her at night-time, as only hourly checks would be what she would get at the surgery. We were told her condition could change so quickly, it would be better to have her with us, so guess what - another night without sleep for me, but Zulu slept soundly.

Next day she went back to be checked out and improvement was obvious. She had a couple of injections and sent away with tablets to take. We were told how lucky we were she had survived the night, it was that serious. Worried that when the injections started to work she would relieve herself of a lot of wind, which would be foul smelling, it wasn't long before we had proof that she was responding to treatment and the vets weren't joking about the smell. In spite of the unpleasantness, it was a joy to see her swollen tummy return to its more normal size. The following day the vets checked her again and were pleased with her. She had improved within a couple of days, much to our relief.

Zulu was her old self and seemed determined to live life to the full. Her diet was changed otherwise walks and play resumed. There was a dark cloud hanging over this recovery period, as the vets did warn us she was quite likely to get a recurrence, and at its worst an operation would be required, but her age was against her to possibly survive. We just settled to enjoy every day with her, and certainly not dwell on possibilities. As the first week passed and the first month, we could easily forget that Zulu had been so ill; she was her old self again.

Somehow she always knew if John was going to be away for the night, as occasionally he was when going to cattle sales in the north of the country. On these occasions, when it got to bedtime, she would go outside for her last trot around the lawn, not only for the obvious, but she would smell the air for any roaming wildlife. Returning to the house she would normally settle down and wait for me to tidy the last cups, and hope she would get a cuddle before I retired to bed. When on my own, she would not leave me as I did the few odd jobs, and as soon as lights went out she would bound upstairs to stay with me all night. She would not even allow Kevin to call me in the morning, and certainly he wouldn't be welcome should he try to enter the room. This protection on my behalf was handed back to John on his return. It never bothers me to be at home alone and could never decide whether Zulu's concern was a comfort or unnerving as she seemed to hold her breath as she listened for a possibly imagined noise, anyway thankfully these nights passed without incident.

She was completely over her illness, and seemed in good health and spirits continuing life as normal. It came as a great shock when four months after her first attack of the twisted gut it was to flare up again. She had had her evening meal and within a quarter of an hour she was giving very loud belching noises, and with hearing the first sound we knew exactly what was happening. Her tummy was swelling up quickly so we gave her the four tablets we had for this sort of emergency, as time was so important to aid recovery. It eased it overnight but she was far from a happy dog by morning. We went to the vets first thing where she was given injections and we were sent home with tablets and had to contact the vet later to let him know her condition. She was no worse, but not the Zulu we knew, but as long as she didn't decline she may respond to the treatment.

My second night was spent with her, although I did get the odd nap with the ear listening for any change in her breathing or movement. She was only eating very little and kept being sick, which was awful. The next evening, definitely restless and not feeling too good, we returned to the vet to discover her temperature had soared to 103 degrees. Treated yet again she and I settled for the third night. She just looked at me whilst I talked to her, until she eventually had a restful sleep.

No change the next day but she was still only eating so little and the sickness wasn't improving. It was whilst spending my fifth night without sleep that I knew, and watched the clock get nearer to the time when it was sensible to contact the vets again, and this time she wouldn't be going for treatment. This last night she had rejected her tablets, and by now the weight loss was obvious, and in my mind it was unkind to put her through any more. The choice of an operation was not advised because of her age when the problem arose previously, and with the aid of drips just to keep her alive we didn't even consider, as a dog just alive but not living is just selfishness in my opinion. As soon as the vet saw her, his decision was the same as ours. Discreetly he disappeared whilst Zulu and I had our last cuddle, and I was yet again able to tell her how much she meant to us all. She may have started our association in the palm of my hand, and she ended it cuddled in my arms.

We never do get used to days like that, and it never gets easier but with the day's work ahead a welcome nights sleep was eagerly awaiting.

Apart from the first two years before we had Tina, I had never known life without at least one dog and this was going to be no exception. With five retired greyhounds we just thought of Anna as the best choice to introduce to the house. She was now nearly eleven years old with weakening legs, and would benefit from the warmth of the house. In the afternoons with Susie they were brought into the house to acquaint themselves to this new environment. Susie was fascinated by the new smells and was curious to inspect all the rooms. Anna was very much more hesitant, and drooped her ears and looked generally miserable. We followed this routine for two weeks but Anna was no more enthusiastic than the first time she entered the house. However, Susie was full of excitement at exploring the new surroundings. Obviously Anna had been kennelled too long to make adjustments, so it was Susie that came to live with us.

On her first night she was washed and dried with a hair dryer, and she wallowed in all this fuss. Clean, fed and tired she laid down on her bed, freshly installed just for her, and soon went to sleep not too far from the comfort of the fire. I knew she would be clean indoors but did wonder about food on a table, whether it would be too much of a temptation. Needless to worry on that count, the thing she had to learn was not to rush around and bump into furniture, and respect windows and glass doors. The windows she took a while to understand and any reflections confused her completely. She just never left my side, which was great company for me.

In no time at all she turned out to be a great guard dog. We have security lights and alarms, which anyone passing, the sensors set off in the house. Susie soon learnt somehow that the sound of the alarm indicated a caller and would go to an appropriate window to witness their arrival. Zulu wasn't a noisy dog but Susie nearly notified the whole county that we had visitors. When one rather undesirable looking fellow called, she was incensed by his appearance, and I'm afraid I'm guilty of doing nothing to quell her desire to escort him from the premises.

Having always been taken on a lead for walks or into grass pens for freedom according to racing days, she learnt to walk around the lawns and garden freely. So far for walks she still goes on the lead, memories of racing are still too vivid and she could take after a cat or rabbit if spotted. The danger of this on open ground is that she would only be intent on the chase, and obstacles or wire fences wouldn't be thought of, and the risk of broken bones would be too great. Maybe as time goes by she will be less bothered about a good chase, but I'm not prepared to chance it yet. I had one or two scary moments when we had been ambling along and a cat crossed our path, with Susie rearing up on her back legs and my arm suddenly one foot longer, it does make one pay attention.

She soon found out that John called me with a cup of coffee and biscuits in the morning, and I would like to think it was me that Susie came to see, but as they both went back downstairs I was left in some doubt as Susie carried a biscuit with her. Her breath sometimes smelt awful and upon inspection revealed some bad teeth. A day at the vets and she returned minus eight teeth and a list of instructions and advice on what to expect in the next couple of days. True she had tablets to ease any discomfort but she tucked into a somewhat slopping mixture of cereal, eggs and very finely mashed meat which rather squashed the second bit of information that your pet may not want to eat for a while. She had shown little interest in the journey, but once out of the car she raced to the door to the house so gone was the advice of keep your dog quiet and no exercise. She did settle down on her bed and slept. Keeping a watchful eye on me just in case I was about to leave her. Next morning she was bouncing about and showed no signs of her previous day's ordeal. Not really appreciating sloppy food but her hunger helped her to overcome her dislike. She was back on duty and warning us of visitors, now had a human had some teeth removed, many would have been complaining. Having spent a day away from home and not the most pleasant one at that, she was going to make sure there was no repeat performance of that for awhile as she stayed even closer to my side and I'm, sure when sleep was necessary it was with an ear and eye on my every move. The greyhounds live to be quite an age generally. Mickey and Anna are now both eleven, Duke and Dawn six and Susie five. We hope to have many years of pleasure still to come.

The latest in the line

Our latest, and last to date, unusual animals to find their way to our farm, are five Highland Cattle and one Longhorn. We were offered them but didn't think about it seriously but a few weeks, later the conversation arose again with the vendor. We asked what their needs were. The price seemed reasonable, so in due course they arrived. As they came out of the lorry they looked like oversized Afghans, as their long hairy coats fluffed about.

We soon got to know their characteristics; they seldom hurry but don't miss a thing that is going on. In the field close to the driveway to the farm, many people have arrived grinning, as they feel as if they have been inspected as suitable to pass through. It was at the peak of the Spice Girls career that the Highlands arrived, and as there was a smaller one, a more ginger coloured one, and one that had so much hair over its face, only to reveal one eye at a time making him look quite scary, so these became the spice boys. We could have sold them many times as everyone likes them, but they are going nowhere for sometime yet.

We have been fortunate with encountering so many different species, some in unusual circumstances. Little did we know that a plea for a dog in the house could

The Spice Boys

lead to such a variety, and so many hours of pleasure gained by just watching their behaviour. With the farm animals we try to ensure that they want for nothing, and are repaid by them strolling up to us to lick us with a very rough tongue, something they wouldn't do if they didn't trust us.

Farm policies at the moment make us consider what we are doing it for, but hopefully before its too late we hope the bureaucrats will give up, and let the true countryman return to the farming ways that have been successful for generations. We would like to finish our working lives with the knowledge we have worked successfully, and should Kevin and Leah wish to continue that they too can enjoy farming as we once did.

As we approach the twilight of our life I hope we shall still have animals around us to give us pleasure, but should for some reason this not be possible, then at least we shall have many happy memories of the ones we have had. We can only feel grateful and thank them all for allowing us into their world and share so much with us.

Thanks

I would like to dedicate this book to the memory of my Mum who's idea it was to write of the various animals. Sadly with memory loss she was unable to understand it.

Thanks have to be mentioned of a friend, Linda Smith, who typed and presented it on disc. Also to Alan Stone and family for preparing it for printing and providing the cover.

Nan Gould